RUNIC
BOOK *of* DAYS

RUNIC
BOOK of DAYS

*A Guide to Living
the Annual Cycle
of Rune Magick*

S. Kelley Harrell

Destiny Books
Rochester, Vermont

Destiny Books
One Park Street
Rochester, Vermont 05767
www.DestinyBooks.com

Destiny Books is a division of Inner Traditions International

Library of Congress Cataloging-in-Publication Data

Names: Harrell, S. Kelley, author.
Title: Runic book of days : a guide to living the annual cycle of rune magick /
    S. Kelley Harrell.
Description: Rochester, Vermont : Destiny Books, 2018. | Includes bibliographical
    references and index.
Identifiers: LCCN 2018002258 (print) | LCCN 2018032268 (ebook) |
    ISBN 9781620557709 (pbk.) | ISBN 9781620557716 (ebook)
Subjects: LCSH: Runes. | Magic.
Classification: LCC BF1623.R89 H37 2018 (print) | LCC BF1623.R89 (ebook) |
    DDC 133.3/3—dc23
LC record available at https://lccn.loc.gov/2018002258

Printed and bound in the United States by Versa Press, Inc.

10 9 8 7 6 5 4 3 2 1

Text design and layout by Debbie Glogover
This book was typeset in Garamond Premier Pro with Elder Futhark, Gill Sans
MT Pro, and Nocturne Serif used as display typefaces

To send correspondence to the author of this book, mail a first-class letter to the author c/o Inner Traditions • Bear & Company, One Park Street, Rochester, VT 05767, and we will forward the communication, or contact the author directly at **www.kelleyharrell.com**.

♦ ♦ ♦

To Kerry
and the power of stories through time.

Contents

Foreword

By Nigel Pennick

Runes have existed in unbroken continuity since their inception more than two thousand years ago. Runic is a time-honored mystical alphabet where each letter has a specific meaning. Each letter embodies an intention laden with deep significance and symbolism that denotes profound connections in the natural world and within the human psyche. Often those who know little about the runes view them as just another means of fortune-telling similar to tarot cards. Indeed, most people come to know the runes through using them as an oracle. But their admirable usefulness in divination is only one small part of their richness. In the *Runic Book of Days* Kelley Harrell explains how, in addition to being a deeply revelatory oracle that gives us insights into present conditions, the runes are also a useful tool for personal growth. Even as an oracle, casting the runes, whose techniques she details in this book, sometimes gives startling results.

The runes first came to prominence in the European spiritual current known as the Northern Tradition in what is now Austria, Germany, the Netherlands, Scandinavia, and England. Although they, like everything else, have a localized origin, they embody the universal principles that underlie existence. Runes emerged from the most fundamental aspects of human life on Earth and the structure and cycles of the Cosmos. They express the core of universal existence.

According to Northern Tradition teachings, the Norse god Odin Allfather, revealer of the runes to the human race, has two attendant ravens called Huginn and Muninn—thought and memory. Each day they fly across the world, observing. These fast-flying birds are symbolic of thought, our consciousness of our being and actions; and memory, our collective history and the sacred observances that are at the root of our being fully human. Everything described by humans must be understandable in human terms, and archetypal symbols embody profound truths. These descriptions, present in the runes, are interpretations of reality according to the innermost structure and function of human consciousness. As Kelley Harrell explains, our most challenging task as humans is finding meaning in self and the world around us. The runes give us a unique means of addressing this existential problem. To those who learn how to use them, the runes can become a spiritual focus that is valuable in our everyday living. Kelley points out that the runes capture the essence of the process of the soul in form, then deliver the wisdom of that story in small, relatable bits. The runes are not an end in themselves. They are a means of achieving personal growth, of embodying spirit through form, of creating manifestation.

Every human spiritual tradition knows that everything takes place in its proper season, in its appropriate time. The old saying "History repeats itself" is a recognition of this. As that sharp observer of human life Mark Twain put it, "By the law of periodical repetition, everything which has happened once must happen again and again—and not capriciously, but at regular periods." Every process in the universe is cyclic, from the rotation of galaxies over vast expanses of time, to the extremely rapid vibration of subatomic particles in fractions of a second. Ancient wisdom taught that each element has its harmonic vibration, which affects us, whether or not we know it. Our direct personal experience is the human cycle of birth, life, and death within the framework of natural cycles of the seasons. Through the runes, we can have a purposeful relationship to Nature through the seasonal round.

Nothing in life and Nature stands still. Every year there is periodical repetition—the equinoxes when daylight and darkness have the same length, and the solstices when the longest and shortest days occur. From midsummer, when daylight is the longest and the night the shortest of the year, the length of days shortens until at the Autumnal Equinox day and night are equal. After the equinox, nights are longer than daylight, until at the Winter Solstice the day is the shortest and the night the longest. After the longest night, daylight again begins to increase, day by day, until the Vernal Equinox, when again daylight and darkness are in equilibrium. Subsequently, days are longer than the nights and increase in length until we are back at the Summer Solstice again. This is the reality of life on Earth.

The solstices and equinoxes have been celebrated for thousands of years and marked with particular rites and ceremonies. Contemporary life, especially in cities, reduces people's awareness of the natural cycles of time. Only national holidays, most of them unrelated to the cycles of Earth and Sun, punctuate an otherwise continuous and hectic schedule. In the city the seasonal sentiment is less apparent than in the country. Between the equinoxes and the solstices are customary sacred festivals derived from European traditional spirituality: the four fire festivals, or "cross-quarter days." They are often called by their familiar Celtic names but also have equivalents in Anglo-Saxon, Norse, and Christian traditions. The equinoxes, solstices, and the four fire festivals make eight festivals in all. Together they mark the turning of the year. These are the sabbats of many contemporary Pagan practitioners, and key initiatory days in this book. Symbolically these sabbats serve to remind us of those who came before us, who were born, lived, and died within the same circling wheel of time in which we find ourselves.

Annual repetition underlies all these spiritual pathways, embedded in the turning of the year. Observing these festivals with runic awareness deepens our relationship to nature and to time. A structured cycle of exercises and meditations, the sequence of initiations explained by Kelley Harrell in this book, enable seekers to repeat them annually on the right day, thereby deepening their experience and awareness at each turn of the wheel of time. "It is necessary to keep up the day" as we say of our ancestral traditions in East Anglia.

The constant cycles that take place in time continually redefine the balance of forces according to their place in the cycle. Each rune corresponds with a particular point in the annual cycle, indicating forces that are in progress at that point in time. The cycle itself is an ever-flowing process, not a fixed state. The dualities expressed in the runes are not competing dualities in a zero-sum game, rather the two opposite parts are two different elements of the same process. One cannot exist without the other: order-chaos, day-night, light-dark, summer-winter, ascent-descent, growth-decline, life-death. Each point in the cycle is a time of transition from one state to the next.

We are all stray singers in the world; things are always changing, and we must live according to the present circumstances. We are engaged in a dynamic interaction with events. The runes as an oracle enable us to elucidate our options for the present and the future. In traditional understanding, luck is viewed not as unpredictable, capricious chance but as a force that ebbs and flows according to cyclic principles. It is often said of successful people that they make their own luck. But rather than directly taking on fate by force, which is impossible, the runes enable us to align ourselves with the ebb and flow of fortune and live life creatively attuned to the cycles of nature in a purposeful way. This gives us limitless possibilities, meaningful results that reveal truths and potentials we could never have thought possible at the beginning of the journey.

As Odin, revealer of the runes, tells us in *Hávamál,* the "Sayings of the High One," "No better load can someone carry on the road than a store of common sense. In unfamiliar places it will seem better than riches."

NIGEL PENNICK is an authority on ancient belief systems, traditions, runes, and geomancy. He is the author of numerous books, including *Runic Astrology, The Complete Illustrated Guide to Runes, The Pagan Book of Days, The Book of Primal Signs,* and *Pagan Magic in the Northern Tradition.* He lives near Cambridge, England, where he follows the oral tradition and Pagan lore of his native East Anglia.

Acknowledgments

Many thanks to the celestially auspicious alignments that helped birth this book.

Thanks to the rune spirits that have sustained me.

Thanks to Natalie Kimber for her bravery and continuous encouragement.

Much gratitude to Nigel Pennick for sharing his scholarship of the runes all these years and for his contributions to this book.

Thanks to the staff of Inner Traditions, particularly Jon Graham, Erica Robinson, Meghan MacLean, and Cannon Labrie.

Thanks for the cheers, support, and grounding love of my family.

Introduction

So in letters of rune on the clasp of the handle
Gleaming and golden, 'twas graven exactly,
Set forth and said, whom that sword had been made for,
Finest of irons, who first it was wrought for,
Wreathed at its handle and gleaming with serpents.
BEOWULF, TRANSLATED BY JOHN LESSLIE HALL[1]

Like so many of you, tenth-grade English literature was my first introduction to the runes. I learned that they were considered a magical alphabet used to conjure, work spells, and imbue objects with power, such as the sword Beowulf used to kill Grendel's mother. In that context, runes were a thing of the past, a relic alphabet of mystics.

It wasn't until I was nineteen years old and in my third year of university that a friend introduced me to them properly. She had the requisite Ralph Blum sack of rune tiles, along with the gilt-edged hard-copy explanatory text. No stranger to divination or woo-woo, I was familiar enough with oracles to know that they didn't work for me. Tarot may as well have presented blank cards. Pendulums froze when I touched them—betraying not even my own pulse. Using ogham, the I Ching, and every other attempt at connecting with the unseen didn't render a scrap of insight for me. My only solid communiqué with the divine came in direct discourse between myself and my spirit guides, who I had encountered from childhood on. It was direct personal experience, and not a specific tradition, that spoke to me. There was an underlying awareness of having been deeply called to stand between worlds all of my life. However, with that faux-velvet bag in hand, I held an intention in mind, plunged my fingers into the cool stones, and drew out magick. My fingers tingled, and the tiles that brushed hot against them were the ones that I cast. To this day, those body sensations are how the runes tell me which ones to draw.

GROWING WITH THE RUNES

The runes spoke to me from our first meeting, and shortly after, I acquired my own set. In all honesty, Blum's take clouded my relationship with them for quite a while. I didn't know enough to realize where his work deviated from more traditionally intact presentations of the staves. I'd touch them, and they'd tingle in my fingers, prodding dormant wisdom. Because my take on them didn't at all jibe with Blum's, and because I knew little beyond classes in world literature about the Old Norse traditions, after a few years of journaling with the runes, I put them down as a formal study. I thought that I was doing something wrong in my work with them, yet couldn't find resources to fill in what was missing. At that time diverse resources on the runes just weren't widely available.

For me it came down to the fact that I just didn't have the confidence to stand in my own relationship with them. I thought that forming such a personal rapport with them was blasphemy to their staid meanings. After all, I'd come from a belief path that didn't allow me to intuit, let alone interpret, my own truth. I had no reason to think Odin would permit otherwise.

Despite tucking them away, the world began presenting itself to me in the context of the runes. They popped up all around—Kenaz in construction signs, Algiz in crisscrossing twigs and branches, Berkano via the Bluetooth symbol—bind runes (ligatures of two or more runes) weaving through my dreams. When I was twenty-seven I began to see runes in my shamanic journeys. That point of direct revelation prompted me to formally pick them back up and never put them down again.

For me the runes are a direct connection to wisdom—that rich infinite pool of awareness tended by the ancients. Where meditation and engaging spirit guides might still leave room for ego to creep in and confuse, with the runes there's room for none of that. They say what they say. They are a wonderful resource to gain insight into all aspects of life, whether through writing them, singing their syllables (called *galdr,* which is both a noun and a verb), or invoking their spiritual manifestations. You can read them for others or incorporate them into ritual items and artwork. You can bring them into every part of your life.

WHAT MY WEIRD ROUTE TO THE RUNES MEANS FOR YOU

I don't want you to have to go through what I did in learning the runes as a modern person far removed from their cultural context. With all the historic resources now available from rune scholars, there's no reason to stumble through anymore. In this book I take my study of those resources and more than two decades of spiritual exploration of the runes and discuss them in a light that is historically informative, culturally appropriate, and presently relatable. Our most challenging task as humans is finding meaning in our self and the world around us, which translates to standing fully conscious in our personal power. I think the runes are a fantastic tool for precisely that, as taken together, they capture the essence of the process of the soul in form, then deliver the wisdom of that story in small, relatable morsels. Who doesn't want that?

As with all of my teaching on energetic and spiritual topics, I'm not interested in preaching a method on how to use the runes. I'm also not going to present my perspective as if it's the gospel according to Freya. It's not. It's mine and only mine. With this book you will come away equally unafraid to explore the runes as you choose, while comfortably aware of how they are traditionally situated and understood. How do I accomplish that? By presenting the staves in a cultural and personal context so that you can create a direct connection with them as you work with them through the seasonal progression of the year. Working through the rituals and initiations of this book, you will learn what, when, where, and why. The how is uniquely you. No matter where you are in your rune studies, this book can affirm for you a foundation to find their wisdom in the world around you and inspire you to become active in shaping how the runes are carried forward on a practical level for us all, from here on. For that reason I maintain that the runes are a viable oracle at any age, at any point on your path. Their tenacious mutability sustains and challenges us.

Being such a clear oracle, the story they tell is our own.

ABOUT THIS BOOK

As I have hinted, my study of the Elder Futhark (the original runic alphabet) has been eclectic, though I approach it from various interpretations of the Old Icelandic, Old Norse, and Anglo-Saxon runic source-poems. My walk with the runes doesn't always encompass traditional views, and I am careful to distinguish these departures throughout the book. In the back I list some resources that cover more conventional takes.

Personally, I approach the runes as part historic evolution of things I love very much—writing and oracle connected by the sacred—and part daily self-exploration tool to become clearer in self-wisdom. My hope is that the runes take root for you in a similar way, inspiring curiosity, mystery, and growth through all seasons.

Where your path differs from mine, go there. I'm not a believer that any one of us knows with certainty what the runes meant in their original context or how they were used. There are different ways to draw the staves and pronounce their galdr. What they mean takes on a different resonance for each of us. This book won't interfere with that personal relationship to the runes. If anything, it should encourage it.

Also, there's no end to the rabbit hole of debate and passion where the runes are concerned. Come into relationship with them and work from there; however, don't be surprised by the number of people willing to tell you you're doing it wrong. I hope this book gives you confidence to at least realize the fallacy of such accusations, if not some foundation to articulate your own logic in response.

Part 1 of this book covers a brief history of the runes, their organization, and their function. Each rune section contains an image of the stave, its galdr, its upright and reversed interpretations (some call them brightstave and merkstave positions), followed by points to consider when working with each. The runic calendar is explained in part 2, as is how our modern observation of the sabbats correlates with the calendar. To help with that, a detailed look at each half-month is followed by a devotional to honor its corresponding rune. These devotionals are preparation for initiations that punctuate each sabbat, whose corresponding half-months utilize the initiation instead of a devotional. These initiations allow you to fully connect with and make use of the life force of each season.

Ultimately, enter this book confident that you can know the runes intimately, and leave it having established a direct relationship with a consistent path to guidance throughout your life.

PART 1
ENGAGING THE RUNES

1

History and Origin of the Runes

I know that I hung
on a high windy tree
for nine long nights
pierced by a spear—Odin's pledge—
given myself to myself.

No one can tell about that tree,
from what deep roots it rises.
They brought me no bread,
no horn to drink from,
gazed toward the ground.
Crying aloud, I caught up runes;
finally I fell.

POEMS OF THE ELDER EDDA,
TRANSLATED BY PATRICIA TERRY[1]

What we know of the runes is as shrouded in mystery as the staves themselves. Their history is uncertain, fraught with much academic debate. We know that they were an alphabet, developed as early as 200 BCE, that was widely used throughout Europe.[2] The oldest inscriptions of the runes are on the Vimose comb and the Meldorf brooch, both dating to the first century CE.[3] Some attribute the runes to Latin origins, while others insist that they are purely Germanic.

What is known is that the Old Norse *rūn* meant "mystery," or "secret sign."[4] Later it came to represent runic characters, an ancient Icelandic set of symbols, which Diana L. Paxson describes as "words of power by which the human intellect is enabled to comprehend the world."[5] These characters are sometimes called staves, which can also refer to sticks (staffs) upon which runes were carved.

The history of their use is as intriguing as their origin and requires a bit of knowledge of Norse cosmology. From the void called Ginnungagap came the Nine Worlds, which carried with them the keys of creation—not just information on how the cosmos was made but a tool available for beings within it to continue shaping it as well. Retrieved by the god Odin when he hung upon Yggdrasil (the World Tree), the runes are these keys. They are the mysteries of the Multiverse—the nine Norse worlds, as well as the internal planes those worlds evoke within us—and Odin was the first being initiated into their magick.

> *It was at the moment that Odin accessed the runes that he took upon himself what I call Urdaic consciousness—the ability to read the records that are stored in the well, on the tree, and in the threads and wood upon which the Nornir record all of existence. Odin's actions allowed a channel for humans and other beings to access the runes, by altering the insular nature of the recording technology.*[6]

Odin's seemingly shamanistic ordeal journeying along the World Tree gave him the runes, which not only enlightened him to their purpose and use but also in how he could convey them to others.

The *Elder Edda*, also known as the *Poetic Edda*, is the definitive resource on Norse mythology, thought to have been recorded between the ninth and twelfth centuries. It contains the *Hávamál*, which is the only account we have of Odin's sacrifice. Snorri Sturluson's thirteenth-century *Prose Edda* revives that mythology for later generations. According to Maria Kvilhaug, Sturluson's work was a secret effort to deliver in poetic code the pagan messages of the Old World to a slowly Christianizing new generation.[7] These works remain our primary sources on how the runes were viewed and used and on the culture that gave them to us.

Many resources give academic blessing to the historical meanings of the runes, some of which present compelling yet conflicting information. Among liberal enthusiasts (often called runesters—I'm not making that up), more traditional scholars, and the Unverified Personal Gnosis (UPG)/Peer-Corroborated Personal Gnosis (PCPG) spiritual seekers, we continue to learn more about the runes in historic application and context as well as how to adapt their wisdom to modern life. As cosmologies and cultures survive by a thread, so do they change and evolve; civilizations rise and fall, yet the runes persist.

In the modern context the runes often are unfairly compared to the tarot. Such a dry comparison immediately reduces them to a mere system of divination, when the runes were and are much more than that. Also, the contemporary mind looks at the countless decks of detailed and lavishly rendered cards that are available now, and internal narratives stir. Recognition of archetypes easily click into place. Most people look at the runes and wonder what the hell those markings are. They are intimidated by the possibility of weaving meaningful stories from them. The truth is, the runes have a lush backstory that modern usage has distilled to single-word meanings. They have been taken so out of context and simplified that they are often avoided and considered too far-out. However, with insight into the Old Norse culture and the runes themselves, it's possible not only to know that rich narrative but also to embody it. The first step in embodying the runes is to remember their roots as an alphabet, then to respect their ancient and cosmic significance.

In this book I present the traditional meanings of the runes in as useful and compelling a modern context as possible. The ancients clearly knew a thing or two, and my approach to the runes maintains that integrity while demonstrating how their wisdom prevails, pervades, and permutates. The power of keeping the runes relevant in a modern context doesn't lie in changing their meaning to suit our contemporary purposes but in finding how their layers of meaning still apply to everyday life.

Given their long and exotic history, the runes continue to challenge conventional thinking, specifically ideologies in which bad and good are presented as opposites, for example, or that light and dark are mutually exclusive. In truth, a working knowledge of Old Norse cosmology can go a long way in unraveling some of the trickier aspects of the runes. It's not required, of course, but who wouldn't want to know more about the main characters in the story of the runes?

THE NINE WORLDS AND THEIR INHABITANTS

From the void of Ginnungagap emerged life as we know it. The creation myth tells us that this "big bang" creation time was the origin of the land of fire—Muspelheimr. Above that lay frosty Niflheimr. Between them was a still meeting point, perfect for the formation of Audhumla (Old Norse: *auðhumla,* lit. "aurochs"), the feminine principle and sacred aurochs who, as far as we know, thought herself into being and freed herself from the ice blocks of the void. The giant Ymir, the hermaphroditic yet masculine principle, was freed from the blocks as Audhumla licked them for sustenance. There are academic discrepancies about which being came first, though the *Eddas* bring some clarity on the subject. Ymir is indicated in both, while Audhumla isn't mentioned at all in the *Poetic Edda.* Despite that omission, she is attested as a critical component of Old Norse cosmology as well as creation. What is clear is that both beings were the result of miraculous elements colliding.

As Audhumla nourished herself on the salty ice blocks, Ymir nursed from Audhumla. What I find most significant about these giants, or Jötnar in the Old Norse mythology, is that, as far as we know, they created themselves. This element of free will, having arisen from the chaos of fiery friction and icy movement, suggests that the unconscious forces that existed in the Multiverse prior to the creation of humanity were transferred through the lineages of Ymir and Audhumla to us.

From Ymir's sweat came other giants. He's also credited with creating the frost giants, a beneficent order of beings who could also be destructive and less-controlled.

Audhumla's form created Buri, the first god, whom some have

equated with Tyr, a namesake of the runic third *ætt* (or family or runes).[8] He had a son called Borr, who married Bestla, a daughter of Ymir's frost giants. Borr and Bestla had three sons: Vodin, Vili, and Ve. This trinity of brothers is often considered to be a reflection of the three qualities of Odin (ecstasy/inspiration, conscious will, and spirit), and through their divine awareness, took up the job of giving order to the universe.

As I mentioned before, the concepts of balance and order are critical to understanding Old Norse culture, largely because they can't be separated from tempering destruction and chaos. Specifically, the ideas of *innangard* and *utangard* stand out. The term *innangard* (Old Norse: *innangarð*) means "inside the gard," or within the ring, while *utangard* (*útangarð/útgarð*) means "outside the gard," or beyond the pale, in more common parlance. These delineations of space indicate what is safe and known versus what is unknown and unknowable, what is tame versus what is wild.

As the gods evolved from the giants, so distinctions were drawn, and these two different lines of beings came into conflict. Though the reason for this dissention isn't explicitly cited in the ancient texts, we can assume it was because each group embodied very different dispositions, possibly divergent outlooks on how the evolving cosmos should continue. The frost giants of Ymir self-identified as Jötnar, and Audhumla's offspring became the Æsir—the group known as gods, though *æsir* loosely translates as "pillars who support the world."[9] While the Æsir saw itself as conduits between bigger, deeper wisdom of the Multiverse and focused on bringing that into form, the Jötnar were the raw, uncontrolled forces of Nature, some more destructive than others. Æsir were innangard, while Jötnar were utangard. These opposing forces represented order (Æsir) and chaos (Jötnar).[10] They didn't necessarily get along, though they respected the role each other played in maintaining balance.

Over eons they fought until finally the trinity of brothers killed Ymir and from his body created the remainder of the Nine Worlds, all connected by Yggdrasil. The Æsir also created the first man and woman, Ask and Embla—with distinct biological gender identities, unlike many other Norse dieties—echoing balanced duality. Asgard was created as the home of the Æsir, with the human domain of Midgard watched over closely by the gods. These were realms of innangard. All else was considered beyond the ring, thus utangard.

The cosmology of the Nine Worlds is filled with many beings, ranging from giants (called *thurses,* Jötnar, or devourers), gods, humans, dark elves, light elves, and dwarves, covering all kinds of terrain. Not considered static, the cosmology, its inhabitants, and significant landmarks are generally referred to with the following correspondences.

Asgard—Home of the Æsir (celestial deities, gods, orderly culture, higher consciousness)

Vanaheimr—Home of the Vanir (land/nature-focused deities, common sense)

Alvheimr (sometimes called Ljossalfheim)—Home of the light elves (logical reasoning)

Niflheimr—Home of the frost giants (power to overcome obstacles)

Midgard—Home of humans

Svartalheimr—Home of the dwarves and dark elves (creative manifestation)

Muspelheimr—Home of the fire giants (blunt and pervasive transformation)

Bifröst—The Rainbow Bridge connecting/separating Midgard from the realms of the gods

Helheimr—Home of the dead (ancestors, intuition)

Jotunheim—Original home of giants (chaotic power, deep consciousness, raw survivalism)

Urd's Well—Home of the Nornir sisters, Urd, Verdandi, and Skuld, (vessel of wyrd, or *urðr* in Old Norse, at the base of the tree)

Mimir's Well—Home of Mimir (vessel of all wisdom, at the base of the tree)

Whether used for the self or in service to others, the runes continually reflect the collective in the individual, the unknown in the known, and the personal embodiment of the unknowable in All Things—the aspect of mystery in Nature that we also embody. This heart of mystery is the crux of the spiritual path based in Old Norse cosmology. Likewise this cosmology isn't a static thing of the past; rather it's a living, evolving worldview, and its inhabitants are very real and engaging. To say the beings of these realms cycle between pleasantry and war with each other is an understatement and is likely colored by what sources one reads or which collective of heathenry one asks. Cyclic warring blurs what exactly is good and bad and yields a gray area, possibly for the sake of neutrality and keeping things balanced but also with the understanding that all things are connected and can't be separated from each other. The Old Norse cosmology gives us the awareness that while lightness may bring enlightenment, it is the darkness that initiates change. While battle may determine who gains control, the ability to blend with rather than wipe out the qualities of the losing culture indicates victory. Old Norse culture made great display of both sides taking hostages, as a show of shared cultural wisdom, for the survival of both civilizations. This sharing of resources indicates acquisition of new knowledge and assures survival.

A detailed knowledge of Old Norse history isn't required to study the runes, though it helps tremendously. A short list of suggested readings for further study about the history and mythology can be found at the back of this book.

The idea that our cosmology continues to change as we evolve in our spiritual studies and that we play a role in intentionally shaping it lies at the heart of the runes; thus, they are our deepest instruction for creating the self. The runes remain a viable tool for personal growth, as well as a deeply revelatory oracle detailing the present and elucidating options for how to best go forward into the future.

2
The Runs

Tools and Strategies for Rune Work

As this book is based on working with the runic calendar, it isn't necessary to have a set of runes on hand. That said, having a set would be a great way to deepen the connection both to the staves themselves and to their seasonal insights. There's something to be said for the act of holding and feeling them, of creating a tactile relationship to the staves. Creating a personal relationship with them in every way possible builds the foundation for working with them through the seasons.

Most rune enthusiasts work with them in very specific yet highly personal ways. They employ rituals to initiate contact with them, create a certain atmosphere in which to use them, and contemplate their intention for using them. To determine the best way to relate to them, consider what aspects of using them feel most important to you.

TOOLS

Runes

Many runesters insist that proper runes must be carved into wood. Others carve or paint them onto stone, bone, or other natural materials. I've known enthusiasts who paint them onto leaves for a specific runecast then offer them to fire after the reading. As with all ritual tools, I suggest using what resonates with you. The materials used—as well as color choice, shape, and any detail significant to the creation of the staves—should reflect your personal bond with them.*

I made my set many years ago. I thought too that proper runes must be carved from wood. However, each time I sat down to do it, the process felt wrong. For me the colors were more significant than the matter, and I settled on metallic-silver clay, with carved staves rendered in cerulean-blue paint.

It's not necessary to make a set of runes. It is, however, a magickal undertaking, and I highly suggest doing it. The process of making them deepens one's relationship to each stave, each ætt, and the entire futhark. If you're not up to making your own set, it should be possible to find an ethically, artisanally crafted one no matter where you are in the world.

Cloth

Many runesters work upon a casting cloth. Creating this boundary between the sacred and the every day (innangard versus utangard) is a common practice in most forms of spiritual or ritual work, though it isn't required. The cloth should be large enough to cover an ample area for the cast but not so big that the runes aren't easily reached after the throw. The cloth may or may not have a pattern drawn onto it that serves as the ground for the casting; such patterns might indicate the cardinal directions or be divided into regions denoting past, present, and future. There are many variations for casting-cloth patterns; their usefulness helps delineate areas for a predetermined variable, such as the past, or relating to some aspect of cosmology, such as any runes

---

*In modern speak and throughout this book the terms *rune* and *stave* are used interchangeably. However, in academic notes and some cultural contexts of reading the runes for divination they are distinct. The characters are staves, as are sticks they may be carved into for magickal purposes. Runes carved into stones or bone are considered "tiles," while runes carved into sticks are "staves." The effect when reading tiles is that you can only read the character on the tile. When reading staves (carved sticks) you can read the character carved into the stick and also the form of the staves or sticks themselves as they fall. So *staves* equates to the symbols, sticks they were carved into, and also to some degree how they're read on sticks in divination.

falling in the east correspond to matters of beginnings, of building life force. I created an oracle cloth specifically for chakra work in which each chakra is represented by a color band. Chakral concerns are read according to the colors the runes fall on. Imagination is the limit when creating a structure for how you work with the runes and how the cloth can help establish that.

Unless I have an intention requiring me to do so, I don't use a cloth that has a pattern. I do, however, use a cloth each time I cast. As the staves fall I observe how far apart they lie and intuit their relationship to each other—if any.

Bag or Box

Storage of the runes is as important as how they're made and used. They should be secured, protected from the elements and damage, easily transportable, and quickly retrievable. For some a drawstring pouch serves well. Others are confident keeping them in a wooden box or other container dedicated only to the safekeeping of the runes. I keep my most-used set in a velvet pouch, stored in a wooden box that I created specifically for that purpose.

Paper and Pencil

Regardless of how we come to study the runes—in a class, from a book, with a mentor, or on our own—the ability to note patterns and trends in casting is very important. For this reason I suggest keeping a rune journal. Draw the spreads and casts, detail the intention for the reading, and make copious notes from the story the runes tell.

Over time meanings may become refined. Some significances may dim, while others stand out. How our relationship to these meanings evolves is important, though it's only applicable if we can remember where we started. Take careful notes, and keep them nearby for reference during casts.

Fetishes

As your work with the runes deepens it may become important to bring fetishes, or power items, into rune sessions. These may take the form of photographs, figurines, crystals, or specific music—whatever feels right in creating the space to honor your engaging with the runes. In shamanism, working with fetishes not only strengthens the relationship to them but also allows the spirits of those items to help create the space for sacred work to be done.

READING RUNES

Drawing

Drawing runes means to blindly select them from a receptacle and place them on the reading cloth. Depending on the intention, there may be a predetermined order for how they are placed on the cloth. Once all the runes are laid out, the reading can be done. Some runesters read as they go, detailing each stave as it's laid out, then summarizing the relationship among all of them after the last rune is put down.

Casting

To use the casting method, blindly withdraw the requisite number of runes for a reading, shake them in cupped hands, then toss them gently onto the reading cloth. Casting can also be done by letting all of the runes fall from their container onto the cloth. Runes that fall outside the designated areas (those areas that indicate cosmological or time-frame significance) on the cloth's design are removed. Runes that fall completely off the cloth are sometimes removed as well. Depending on the intention and personal eccentricities regarding the layout, the runes are then read.

Spreads

Predetermined arrangements or configurations of the runes, in which each position has a unique meaning that contributes to the overall story of the reading, can also be used. There are some more common spreads, such as Odin's Rune, which is a single rune layout; a two-rune spread (called by many names), indicating the present and that which becomes; or a three-rune spread (also known by many names), which indicates past, present, and future. Some spreads use up to nine runes, while very industrious runesters create elaborate spreads that use all of the staves.

Truly the sky is the limit in creating rune spreads. As long as they have meaning that is applicable to life, working with various spreads is a valuable way to have a personal relationship to the runes and learn about how they relate to each other within the specified contexts. By using predetermined spreads we don't have to hold as tightly to constructing the links between the runes. The spread creates that synergy for us, and we can focus more on how the staves inform us about our intention.

Positions

There's no historical precedent for working with the runes in any other than the upright (or brightstave) position. Because the runes were first an alphabet, for many runesters reading reversed (facing upward, though upside down), merkstave (face down), or in opposition (atop another rune) are blasphemous practices. For that reason, reading only upright positions seems truer to their cultural context. Be prepared, however, for strong arguments in rune communities regarding positions and which are most appropriate. I suggest knowing the rune meanings quite well upright before factoring in reading reversals, if at all. Initially I was a prescriptivist and didn't read reversed meanings. After doing many readings for others and seeing life dynamics in which specific runes presented as reversed, I began incorporating reversals into my interpretations.

That said, the practice of reading other positions has evolved in great detail. It's easy to see that some staves can be reversed while others cannot. Runes that can't be reversed remain right-side up no matter how they're positioned. Interpreting positions may seem like splitting hairs to some enthusiasts, while others wouldn't cast without noting every detail of how the staves fall. It's a personal thing, really. Go with how they speak to you.

Work with the runes, touch them, sense your connections with each one. Develop a relationship to the method that best works—using set spreads, draws, or loose casts. Within that method, get a feel for the significance of stave positions and their implications for readings.

The possible positions are:

* **Brightstave**—Upright, and/or facing upward
* **Merkstave, or murkstave** (*myrkstafr* in Old Norse)—Face down, or outside the allotted casting area
* **Reversed**—Upside down, though facing upward
* **Opposition**—Atop each other in a blind cast

Some practitioners work with a position called "converse," which usually refers to the primary stave quality being hidden, or not consciously realized for what it is. For me that meaning is covered in the merkstave position.

Likewise the positions may factor into interpretation. For instance:

* **Brightstave**—The face-value meaning
* **Merkstave**—That which is occluded, hidden, shadowed
* **Reversed**—The current struggle
* **Opposition**—The "on-its-way" dynamic

What's most important to understand about rune positions other than upright is that they are erroneously considered negative or dark. I've talked with a lot of people who comment on the runes feeling shadowy compared to other forms of divination. I think that interpretation comes from not understanding that in Old Norse culture these concepts of good and bad didn't exist as discrete or isolated from each other. The two sides of a coin are ultimately still the same coin, conjoined and always working in tandem. Embracing that nuance will go a long way in clarifying the runes.

For me position is more about the stave telling me what life force is flowing well, what needs attention, and what needs total resuscitation. Generally speaking I find that the complexity of interpreting positions depends on how detailed I want the reading to be. For instance, when I draw one rune I'm more likely to read brightstave as "go for it" and merkstave as "not at this time," though in a fuller spread I take the position into deeper consideration. The position may indicate an order of operations in the reading or hint at the present point in a cycle. In a cast, a close distance between runes would indicate that the time is now, whereas if they fell far apart I'd read that as occurring over a longer duration, and perhaps some clarifying staves would need to be drawn to fill in the progression.

Brightstave indicates to me that the life force of that unique rune is moving as it should be in the stated intention. Merkstave informs me of unconscious motivations, while reversed indicates where life force has ebbed and needs attention. Staves in opposition, such as one rune lying over another, may indicate that the state of the top rune must occur before the bottom one, or that the top rune holds the underlying one back in some way. In some cases runes in opposition may present a conjoined relationship in which one can't manifest its purpose without the other.

Interpreting the meaning of individual runes, or a spread, or a cast, may seem whimsical with regard to when to factor in positions. It would be more accurate to say that interpreting them is intuitive. Certainly the interpretations of the staves retain their traditional meaning even with the nuances of modern life laid over them. Being able to draw out their story within the framework of a specific intention is nothing less than an intuitive undertaking born of one's personal relationship to the runes and one's method of reading their significances.

Interpretation is highly intuitive, greatly subjective, and I encourage approaching the process of reading the runes by what feels right. In this book I offer brightstave and merkstave connections with the runes in hopes that through personal study and engagement the positions will reveal themselves.

With regard to the runic calendar, there is only the brightstave position.

Reading Order

Runes can be read right to left, left to right, or however you prefer. There is no historic precedent on how the runes were literally read. In many cases the runes on ancient artifacts can be read both ways or in a boustrophedon pattern—right to left, then left to right, in alternating lines.

Meaning

Meaning has two roles in working with the runes. Foremost, each rune has a unique meaning or interpretation. Some staves present very specific conditions or dynamics, while others are conditional, mutable. As mentioned above, I will present traditional meanings of the runes along with anecdotes to bring them into a more contemporary context.

The second role of meaning when working with the runes is that they must have meaning *for you*. The work done with them must be valuable, in that it brings meaning to your life; if not, then further exploration of the semantics, positions, methods, or history is necessary. If using a set method, interpretation, or process isn't working, shake it up. If it doesn't bring meaning to your life, something in the mix isn't right. Don't be afraid to change it.

This text is not the be-all and end-all of runes, and it isn't intended to be. Serving as an introduction to possibilities with the runes, it is at best a guidebook that gives readers background on the staves and helps them form their own understandings of these meanings, how the meanings apply to their lives and runecasting, and how to form relationships with the runes. Read many sources. Work with a mentor who is well versed in the runes. Galdr them. Explore other runic systems (there are many). Call in the deities of each ætt, or spirit, of each rune for guidance in working with it. There's no end to the world of study options for the runes, and different approaches color their historic meaning and personal use. Let this book be a beginning for understanding the meaning they can bring into your life.

Worth mentioning here is that I don't work with the modern invention of the blank rune. I recognize that for some the blank allows a certain freedom in working with the runes. My feeling is that the staves as they are cover what territory a blank rune is meant to cover.

GALDR

An Old Norse word for "spell," or "incantation," *galdr* is sounding, toning, or chanting used with magickal intent.[1] It was the gift that Odin gave to humanity. The practice of engaging sound with symbolism is a

pervasive and powerful exercise. As Japanese *kotodama* and Vedic man-
tras indicate sacred lineages of spiritual enlivening through sound and
visual fusion, so the runes invite the same through galdr.

Generally speaking, galdr is the slow repetition of the runic name
in varying vocal tones, with intention focused on the rune's meaning.
The exact pronunciation and intonation of the galdr is not important;
it is the intention behind the sounds that matters. Feeling the vibration
of the rune's sound in the body evokes a trance state. The galdr of each
rune is included in the next chapter.

For me sound creates an energetic connection with the runes, which
has enhanced my understanding of how to use the staves. Because the
runes spread to many cultures over time, how they are pronounced var-
ies. It's okay to practice what sounds produce the resonance needed and
to go off-road if the ones I cite need tweaking.

A good exercise in bonding with the runes is to sing them. Try
different pronunciations and go with ones that flow through your
body. Note what sensations are stirred, what feelings, thoughts, and
memories arise. Observe where in the body energy is stirred by specific galdr. After all, the primary story of the runes is that of spirit
moving through form, imagination creating manifestation, and all the
wild experiences in between. I've found that the more I speak them in
ritual and discuss them aloud in work with others, the more deeply I
connect with them.

THE RUNE KEEPER

My work in this plane must be animistic, or I'm not doing it to my
fullest capacity. In my worldview everything has a soul, and because I
hold that truth I am obligated to engage that soul when I work with
its physical counterpart. For that reason I suggest calling in a guide—
the guardian of the runes, a rune keeper, the soul, or some spiritual
expression of the keeper and his or her infinite wisdom—to facilitate
your work with the staves. That may be inviting in the soul of the Elder
Futhark or creating a relationship with the souls of each stave or of
some ancestral or multiversal rune master. For me it's a combination of

these, all mediated by Heimdallr, the guardian of the Rainbow Bridge between Midgard and Asgard.

If you feel compelled to ask a specific significant figure from the Old Norse culture to act in this capacity for you, this interaction can go a long way toward deepening your connection with the overall context of the runes. Many work with Odin, Freya, the Norns, Yggdrasil, or some other lineage ancestor. This interaction can be as simple as asking this being to come in before you work with the runes. You could invite this being into your overall spiritual practice by singing to it daily or creating altar space for it. However you feel led to work with a spiritual teacher, consider making that gesture at this point in your rune study.

THE ELDER FUTHARK

As I mentioned above, there are many runic systems. The first of these, and the one used in this book, is the Elder Futhark. It contains twenty-four staves, and its name comes from the first six runes: *f u th a r k*. The runes are traditionally grouped into three groups of eight. Other well-known futharks—the Anglo-Saxon Futhark (also called Anglo-Frisian Runes) and Scandinavian Younger Futhark—are based on the Elder Futhark. Because there are few remaining references to the Elder Futhark, most of what we know of it has been learned through our study of the later futharks. For instance, we don't really know how the rune names were pronounced in the Elder Futhark. What we have is a best guess, which results in different pronunciations and spellings for the runes. I have noted the ones most commonly used in this book.

This order and grouping of the twenty-four runes is the tradition-ally accepted organization of the Elder Futhark. However, there are compelling arguments for arranging the staves differently. Some put Uruz first, while traditionalists begin with Fehu. Others insist that Dagaz is the final rune in the third grouping, with Othala being second to last. I wholly advocate studying different organizations of the runes; in the different orderings the overall story the runes tell changes, as do the individual interpretations of each rune.

THE ÆTTIR

The runes are divided into three *ættir* (families), creating three sets of runes with eight in each ætt. Each ætt is named for the first rune in the group. This division is largely derived from what seems to be the evolu-tion of the staves. In that evolution each ætt indicates a unique func-tion, if not series of challenges, each culminating in completion of a cycle before beginning again. In other words, as each stave is an element of the rune story, each ætt gives us clues as to what challenges lie ahead. One rune to the next, and certainly one ætt to the next, everything that was learned is challenged.

Frey's Ætt
Frey's Ætt is the first, thus it is the oldest.

ᚠ ᚢ ᚦ ᚨ ᚱ ᚲ ᚷ ᚹ

It's named for Frey (Old Norse: *Freyr*), the Æsir god of growth, prosperity, and fertility—all aspects of wealth and healthy living. The twin of god-dess Freya of the Vanir, who originated the shamanic practice of *seiðr* (Old Norse, magickal techniques), the two are referenced separately in stories though are often conjoined as masculine/feminine equals. Thus it isn't unheard of for the first ætt to also be attributed to Freya, who embodies the qualities of nurture, working with the wyrd, and also fertility.

Often *wyrd* is mentioned in the same context as luck, fate, or des-tiny, though it's more complex than those. In its cultural context, wyrd is symbolized as a tapestry of threads, some of which we have control over, some we don't. For example, our poor past deeds are done, as are those of our ancestors. We can't change them, and they do impact our standing in the present. As such, we can take responsibility for both, and in doing so behave more in alignment with what we want or need in the present. How we modify our acknowledgment of and engagement with threads of the past changes our options for threads in the present. This is wyrdweaving in a simple form. A more complex form could involve shamanic healing of ancestors or releasing curses. These and other threads form the personal and collective tapestry of wyrd.

The first ætt deals with discerning the threads we control from those we do not and learning how to wyrdweave, or change, what we can. Thus its mastery includes brewing our thoughtforms into actionable desires and coming into the revelation of ourselves as gods, goddesses, divinity. Associated with the giants and the primal life force that predated them, this family of staves advances us from a sense of need and yearning to gestating the soul into flesh. It moves us through finding and creating deep self-nurture yet realizing that a world beyond such safety beckons. With these runes we set up our ability to be human.

This ætt is deeply connected to a facet of Odin called inspiration and our path to how to become inspired, how to stay inspired, and what to create from it.

Heimdallr's Ætt

The second ætt is Heimdallr's Ætt, sometimes called Hagal's Ætt.

ᚺ ᚾ ᛁ ᛃ ᛇ ᛈ ᛉ ᛊ

Keeper of the Bifröst Bridge, also called the Rainbow Bridge, Heimdallr stands between the domains of gods and goddesses (Asgard) and humans (Midgard). In short, he is the link between gods and humanity. He protects divinity, thus order, by keeping gods and humans distinct.

As a warrior Heimdallr assures that we meet certain conditions befitting mastery before we are permitted access to higher consciousness. However nontraditional the correlation may be, the overlap between this function of Heimdallr's Rainbow Bridge and that of the chakra system (in Old Norse: *hvels,* "wheels") stands out to me as significant in the development of human awareness. As such, the theme of this ætt involves moving through life experiences and, despite tribulation, thinking them through alongside our divine origins, while retaining some sense of divinity. It's about the trials of realizing that we are souls in bodies, forced to deal with the sticky, messy realities of formed being. As such, the sophomore year isn't easy.

Heimdallr's is the hero's journey, very much between states. His is the realization that we are human and god and that the tension between those two characterizes our entire experience in form. We may acquire the wisdom of gods, though we will still have to cope with human trials.

This ætt is connected with another facet of Odin (his brother, who is sometimes called Vili or Hoenir), which is will, our ability to take inspired action.

Tyr's Ætt

Tyr's Ætt is the third and final rune grouping.

ᛏ ᛒ ᛗ ᛙ ᛚ ᛜ ᛞ ᛟ

As Tyr, sometimes interchanged with Tiwaz, we undertake the path of the sage. At this point we glean wisdom from the creation-manifestation dramas of the first two ættir and realize that's life—warts, gems, and all; it's what we get, and our perspective on our experience largely determines what we do with its wisdom.

Through understanding the mysteries of the Multiverse revealed in this ætt, we experience the sacrifice of the self for the betterment of tribe, and we find victory—only to realize there's another battle. The strength of this ætt is that despite wear and tear we find the ability to stand in the center of that cyclic truth.

This ætt is also connected with a facet of Odin (his brother, who is sometimes called Vé or Lodurr), which is holiness, or our ability to take passion and manifest it in our lives, to go on, to persevere.

3

The Staves

The Symbolism of the Elder Futhark

FIRST ÆTT

In this chapter we take each rune, one by one, and examine its significance. The information of each is broken down into seasonal dates (or half-months), pronunciation, galdr, meaning, then reversed meaning—where applicable. The seasonal dates are based on the work of Nigel Pennick, whose book *Runic Astrology* laid the foundation for the modern runic calendar. Part 2 of this book goes into further detail about the history and application of the seasonal dates.

It's important to note that the pronunciation of the Elder Futhark runes is a guess at best. No one is completely sure how they were pronounced. The way we commonly pronounce them is based on documented information from later futharks and texts that reference the Elder Futhark, though written long after its use.

Likewise how we galdr the runes and arrive at their meanings is an open study. As with the pronunciation, galdr of the Elder runes is largely based on Anglo influences. As mentioned earlier, for the purposes of this book the importance of the galdr lies in its intention, not in how you pronounce or intone the syllables and sounds. Sound each galdr in whatever way feels right to you.

Regarding meaning, we know conceptually what some of the runic characters meant, though some meanings are widely contested. Where the Old Norse meaning of the rune is known, I have noted it for each, with care to note the English translation. In most cases the direct translation is rudimentary, while the indirect translation draws on cultural and timing elements, which focus on fuller dynamics encompassing the literal translation. The indirect translations focus on how we experience the literal translations, which makes them more applicable to modern life. Ultimately the runic names come from an amalgam of different regional cultures and languages across time, which makes translating them into English further problematic.

Exploring the first ætt, we identify the need or gift we bring to the world. Let us embark on a journey through Frey's Ætt from Fehu to Wunjo.

Fehu

Stave symbol: ᚠ
Half-month dates: June 29–July 14
Pronunciation: *feh-hoo*
Galdr: *fee-hoo*

Fehu (lit. "cattle"): Wealth. The first stave of the Elder Futhark, Fehu, is where it all begins. Literally translated as domesticated "cattle," this stave is generally regarded to mean "wealth," or that which we must tend to keep assets bountiful and healthy. The ability to tend assets first of all calls to mind that there is something to tend; thus it affirms the responsibility required to care for movable wealth. If we reflect on the significance of cattle to Old Icelandic culture, it is easy to see why those animals were the currency of the time. The trading of domesticated cattle forged bonds, generated sustenance, gave shelter. It was the embodiment of energy exchange. It was the "fee" of the day, and as such is the origin of the English word "fee."

The realm of what can be accomplished with wealth is also the domain of Fehu. It represents primal power that we all hold to either consciously or unconsciously shape the world around us. As the initial rune of the futhark, it posits that we must be able to provide for ourselves. We must be able to take the resources we're given and do something beneficial with them. At heart it teaches that we can't just be born and be handed everything. We must ground ourselves well as spirits in form and develop a relationship with work and the randomness of having and losing.

Some characterize Fehu as feminine, while others find it masculine. Regardless, when Fehu presents itself, pay attention to the mundane plight and secure your assets. Before we can venture far and beyond into spiritual subjects, we must be well grounded in our everyday needs, desires, and opportunities. When we take care of our house so that we have a firm foundation, we create the strength and opportunity to fulfill our heart's desires and stand powerfully in community.

The challenge of Fehu is to find spiritual wealth as a soul embodied in flesh.

Reversed

Reading Fehu reversed is fairly straightforward: when upside down, possessions fall out of our pockets. Maybe that's figurative; perhaps it's literal. What's certain is the frustration of the efforts of hard work falling through our fingers and the refinement of focus from a dangling carrot to what assets are really needed at this time. Just as we tend what we gain, we must also tend the lack in what we've lost. *Tending* and *spending* are the watchwords of Fehu reversed. We must bring life back to the basics.

Uruz

Stave symbol: ᚢ
Half-month dates: July 14–July 29
Pronunciation: *oo-rooz*
Galdr: *urr-uz*

Uruz (lit. "aurochs"): Nature or primal nature. It's telling that the first rune indicates everyday cattle, or basic needs being met, while the translation of the second, Uruz, is "aurochs," a gigantic, untameable, now-extinct creature. In the Old Norse cosmology Audhumla is the feminine principle, the auroch that nourished life into being. She is ice that engages fire to ignite life. (In Old Norse cosmology, there were only two elements—fire and ice—which combined to create life.) This stave marks our first step into the mysteries of personhood and thus represents a rite of passage into the mysteries of Nature and form.

Since Audhumla was the feminine principle embodied as an aurochs, Uruz brings with it the realization that we are primal, we are Nature. Thus, when Uruz turns up in a cast, something wild is about to happen. As we become aware that we are part of raw life force, we become aware of our ability to shape the Multiverse. We brush against Nature's mysteries, specifically the fact that we're one of them.

Progenitor of the giants, then the Æsir and all of life that followed, Audhumla was the Divine Mother, the sacred cow of the Old Northern Tradition.* Where the tamed cattle of Fehu *does*—it is brute action and force and symbolizes the primordial fire that sparked All Things—Uruz *is* the icy, wild, primal aurochs that embodies form, sustains that divine spark, and gives it focus. Between these runes we learn that action and embodiment are required forces of life. One requires the other for progression to occur.

As part of the forces of Nature that don't mess around—by which I mean the giants in Old Norse cosmology—Uruz is often associated with the feminine aspect of the creative process. Uruz sounds very earth-goddessy and potent on the surface, though deeper than that is its penchant for keeping unchecked motivations outside the lines. Yes, I said *outside* the lines.

Uruz comes up when we're living too tidily. Consider Audhumla the bedrock of thoughtform + desire + drive = manifestation. She is the original creative force that thought herself into being through active will and is the application of all that she was to generate herself as she wanted to be.

Without that drive and desire to carry the thoughtform through to the finish, we're just daydreaming. Uruz is pedal-to-the-metal engagement, direct relationship, intentional animism lived out loud. She is unconscious motivation realized and come to fruition.

---

*The Northern Tradition/Path is a general phrase that can include Asatru, Vanatru, Heathen, or an undefined Old Norse–influenced modern spiritual path.

Aurochs were wild, if not untamable. The not-so-modest hint here is that we should be too, or at least be in touch with this side of ourselves. We ride a fine line between finding the life and community that can give us that affirmation, yet also honoring our wildness. When we aren't in touch with our wild sides, seemingly abrupt upheavals throw us off course when really we just weren't open to the signs leading up to change.

So no, Uruz isn't the cross-your-legs and look pretty kind of feminine. It's the savage soul story "lived out loud or die" kind of feminine. In that sense, it reminds us to find the balance of what's required of us, and what's *really required of us*. Brightstave or merkstave, Uruz brings our needs into sharp focus—or else. Often people find Uruz difficult to communicate or situate into the narrative of a cast, because it's not well conveyed with words or context; rather it's felt.

Every thing that exists harbors a propelling urge to keep going, to be, to progress. It is the mitochondrial quest to survive against all odds. Such is the ferocity of Uruz, as well as its impact upon our psyches. Working consciously with this rune can bring about a deep transformation in how we manifest ourselves, which is to say, how we give meaning to our lives. Uruz indicates a rite of passage into awakened personhood. We are both the mystery and its wisdom. We are the toiling at the work of our lives, the summation of the work of our lives, and how we carry that work into new experiences, all at once. Realizing that we play a role in creating ourselves is one thing. That we embody that role while we toil is another.

Such is the challenge of Uruz: our first opportunity to bring the unconscious into consciousness. When we encounter this rune we aren't only engaging base primal forces, we *are* them.

The challenge of Uruz is to see the self as naturally empowered.

Reversed

Uruz reversed indicates unconsciously chipping away at some hidden inner power. Generally thought of as our most primal aspect of self—the True Self—Uruz comes when our vitality is challenged, and we're encouraged to go back to our most basic roots and cultivate them to grow deeper. The emphasis is on self-care. Truly, can the roots ever grow deeply enough? Is there ever a point at which our primal support is too much?

Uruz inverted doesn't encourage patching together a crumbling foundation or gnashing teeth to figure out what the block is; rather it fosters remembering that there's always room to grow, that no matter what's going on, the True Self has always been, and still craves light to blossom.

Thurisaz

Stave symbol: þ
Half-month dates: July 29–August 13
Pronunciation: *THOOR-ee-sawz*
Galdr: *t-thur-thir-thor*

Thurisaz (lit. "giant"): Thorn, a catalyst for awakening. This rune tells much about the human journey into form, presenting the point at which we begin to distinguish ourselves as distinct from the Source— not separate from, but distinct from. We are beings of passion, with life force always uniting us with All That Is, which is the setting of Thurisaz.

In Old Icelandic mythology this connection and its power stemmed from the giants (*thurs*), whose primal nature rumbles in us as kundalini and deep unconsciousness, which can simmer or blast us into active participation. Anyone who's worked with kundalini knows that it's volatile stuff, and approaching it with measured finesse wins out over furiously forced success. In runic cosmology giants came first. They made the gods; thus they are the originators of everything that came after.

That said, this rune is connected with primal masculine energy and is related to Thor and his enormous hammer, Mjölner. Maria Kvilhaug suggests that this force is the magnetic field of the planet—that which protects us from utangard. Personified, it is instinct without ego. Where Fehu and Uruz are deeply unconscious, Thurisaz is the liminal micro-thought that just skitters at the edge of awareness. We're aware that something is demanding our attention, though we aren't entirely cognizant of what it is. It is that thin boundary that separates layers of consciousness yet holds them together.

Thor is both that slim consciousness and the slamming realization that a situation long requiring change must happen now. Such power indicates an abrupt modification of events, ultimately for the good, *by our own choosing*. It is the our choice that most defines the forces of Thurisaz. Again, we are dealing with a deep force from within acting as catalyst for change.

It is that choice that distinguishes this rune from the other "change" runes: we have control. We may not like the change, but we're a factor in how it plays out. What makes control actually powerful is knowing what to do with it. In and of itself, control isn't worth much, and having the discernment about how to hold it and enact it effectively delineates whether it's useful. When this stave appears it means we have the choice in how we control ourselves. We can act in a way that still flows with divine order (*örlög*). We can have free will and still stay connected with All Things.

A key note about Thurisaz is that, while it indicates the time to strike, miss the mark and it's over. The moment has passed. Of course the only way to be assured of a wanted outcome is to stay aligned with örlög. And the only way to truly flow with divine order is not to be attached to the outcome.

With Thurisaz comes the thoughtform of awareness of one's self and what one could become. Protect it.

Thus the challenge of Thurisaz is to wield control with compassion.

Reversed

Indeed, Thurisaz is about overcoming the thorns along our path, though it also cautions us to heed the places where pain is inevitable in forward movement. It can't be avoided, though this reversed position indicates that it can be gracefully overcome. As long as we recognize that this is not the time to stubbornly push forward but to breathe in life force and discern the best path for the moment, how we free ourselves from our thorns will leave us better informed and intensely more aware.

Ansuz

Stave symbol: ᚨ

Half-month dates: August 13–August 29

Pronunciation: *AHN-sooz*

Galdr: *aaaa-ahh-an-as-oss*

Ansuz (lit. "god"): Breath. The fourth rune is ascribed to Odin as the creator of Midgard (Earth) in the Old Norse cosmology. What's significant about this attribution is that Odin breathed life into two trees (Ask and Embla) to create the first humans. As a result, this rune is often interpreted as "mouth" or "breath." From that breath humans became animate beings who use breath to ascribe words to concepts. In that progression, through words we too give life. We have stepped beyond the deeper consciousness of the giant life force of the first three staves and have arrived at how we consciously internalize and externalize our souls. With Ansuz we realize the impact we have on the world around us. We learn to interpret and transmit signals.

With this stave we begin to realize the power of speaking; thus we mire ourselves in the murky examination of the thing versus the name we give it. We begin to see how the truth we speak is sometimes not as clear as the one we feel, and the process we go through that results in speech reflects our every truth. Likewise, as we build the language of our formed experience, we become aware that someone is listening to what we say. The knowledge we've been given we then pass on to others. In that way Ansuz is a living, breathing cycle. It is prophetic.

Ansuz calls our attention to that sticky place between inspiration and how it's expressed, between thoughtform and how we empower it. This stave directs us to become aware of our truth and how we put it forward into the world. Of course the precursor to that is listening to our heart's song when it sings so as to discern our sacred duty. The challenge of articulate communication seems easy, though the ability to discern personal truth, let alone carry it out, remains one of the most difficult tasks of the soul in form. To make a more commonly known comparison, if Thurisaz is unbridled kundalini, or creative force, Ansuz is mindfully directed prana, or life force. It is our wildness distilled to our truth, fitted to the acceptable norms of our culture.

For this reason Anuz is considered Odin's rune, or the rune embodying the divine in our lives, presenting wisdom or power soon to be revealed. It reminds us that we are never separate from what has created us or from what we create, so we must create with care.

The challenge of Ansuz is mastering the internal process of choosing what we give attention to—how we present ourselves to All Things.

Reversed

As Ansuz brightstave is connected with Odin; positioned otherwise it carries connotations of Loki, or facts not being as clear as they seem. The appearance of Ansuz reversed doesn't mean that things are bad or out to deceive; rather it cautions us to go further into self to determine how to proceed. It isn't a judgment on the situation. It's a call to appeal to intuition over opinion, or even the facts. In this way we need to consider whether we're speaking in truth and listening in earnest.

Raidho

Stave symbol: ᚱ
Half-month dates: August 29–September 13
Pronunciation: *RIDE-ho*
Galdr: *ridhe-rithe*

Raidho (lit. "ride"): Travel. Many people read Raidho in a very literal context, meaning a journey between two points, emphasizing the mode of transportation involved, movement across space and time, and everything that occurs between origin and destination. Indeed, that's the stuff of our most compelling stories.

On a spiritual level, with Raidho we begin to understand how our choices affect All Things and how our ability to sustain long-term focus while holding the details loosely informs the story we tell of ourselves, of our lives. Anytime Raidho appears in a cast I pause, because it draws on all the things most vital to me: words, travel, and the interconnection of All Things. In short, Raidho indicates how we tell our story.

Sometimes to best understand a rune, examining those runes framing it gives it deeper context. The journey of the runes in the first ætt is about inspiration becoming form for the first time; thus it emphasizes the realization of self-empowerment through connection with All Things. Before Raidho comes Ansuz, in which we begin ascribing words to concepts. Following Raidho is Kenaz, torch, presenting the complex experience of sudden awareness, the spark that ignites, the aha moment. It is the moment in which meaning is derived from our experience.

With that fuller understanding in mind, let's revisit Raidho.

Inspiration + Storytelling = Meaning
Ansuz + Raidho = Kenaz

The concept is oversimplified, but it conveys the meaning well. Raidho clarifies the importance of holding focus over duration, associating a starting point and result with every choice, decision, thought, and deed committed along the way.

We're told all the time how life isn't about the outcome but the journey. I'm pretty sure Raidho says that it's a delicate balance of both. Ultimately, how we think and express our perspective not only shades our cosmology and how we see self and the world, but it to some degree creates it. This stave embodies the process of culling out how much of ourselves we share with the world, realizing the impact of sharing, and deciding what we should hold only for ourselves.

The challenge of Raidho is staying with the journey, even if the map changes.

Reversed

Given its propensity to indicate a journey, literally and figuratively, Raidho merkstave doesn't mean "Don't go there"; rather it holds all plans very loosely—the map, route options, pit stops, itinerary, and of course, destination. While we can't control every facet of how our story is shaped, we can control how we respond to how it becomes edited. Things are not going to go as planned, and coping with that as well as possible is foremost.

Kenaz

Stave symbol: ᚲ
Half-month dates: September 13–September 28
Pronunciation: *kehn-naz*
Galdr: *ken-keen-kon-ki-kee*

Kenaz (lit. "torch"): Illumination/Kenning. In the younger futharks Kenaz speaks to the fire we can control, the torch of inspiration we both nurture and bring into being as wisdom. This esoteric moment is the lighting of the darkness. In practical terms it's the illuminating match strike in an otherwise pitch-black cave. It's the aha moment of the soul. We call such a moment divine, in which we stand fully and knowingly connected to All Things. We completely hold our power.

Kenaz calls us to examine the flame in our lives. On the surface it seems easy to recognize the places that are lit, particularly when we explore what is most dark. Even the tiniest flicker blazes bright and illuminating when we're surrounded by total darkness.

This stave usually comes at the close of wandering (Raidho, yes?) and sheds insight into how we manifest. Bear in mind, manifesting isn't really about bringing something into being. It's true emphasis is on how we react to the inspiration. Often we have enlightenment, but we don't like what's learned or how it makes us feel. Nonetheless, we can't unknow it. We can't revert back to who we were before wisdom, not without creating a landslide of ramifications. Kenaz puts us front and center to both the enlightenment and the tension it brings to needed change in our lives.

Regarding that tension, in the Old Icelandic traditions this rune references a "boil," or more specifically a blemish—that which is inflamed and swollen. It is also related to keening, or lamenting. Often this meaning is overlooked in favor of the brighter "torch." I think there's not only room for both but that they are connected.

Another understanding of Kenaz is kenning, or the bringing together of two seemingly unrelated words or concepts, such that when combined new awareness is formed. Usually based in a literal and metaphoric fusion, such as the term *battle sweat,* meaning "blood," in *Beowulf,* kennings take common ideas and route them through provocative unconscious symbolism. Contemporary kennings are *rug rats* and *tree hugger,* both of which clearly identify what they describe and also evoke feelings about them. With this meaning, Kenaz calls us to think differently, to reorganize mental structures around a deeply unconscious awareness that wishes to be known.

Often when we receive enlightenment it comes with searing pain, because growth is demanded, ego is chapped, change is imminent. The appearance of Kenaz can indicate sore spots that need to be revealed, places where we need to think and respond differently. Perhaps what makes them most sore is the fact that we were already aware of them and didn't want the conflict they would bring. Whatever the source of revelation, however challenging it may be to process, it won't overwhelm. One of the hallmarks of this stave is small, digestible bits of insight, revealed as needed or as processed. Kenaz brings a wonderful opportunity to take stock and make wanted changes.

The challenge of Kenaz is finding the light in the shadows and letting the shadows stay lit.

Reversed

Reversed, Kenaz is a speck of light in pitch dark—not exactly lit, but not totally oblivious either. In this position we must be comfortable with darkness, or at least flickers of it. To bring greater light we must let go of what is no longer needed.

Kenaz reversed can also indicate the suffering of secret pain; a buried hurt is a motivating fire, all its own. So often we register discomfort in our lives, and we don't know where it's coming from. Kenaz reversed shows us, vividly. It circumvents the mystery and lays bare to the light what's going on. Our job is to have the fortitude to collect the ash left from the flame and dispose of it appropriately.

Bless it. Thank it. Love it, and let it move on to its destiny.

Gebo

Stave symbol: X

Half-month dates: Septmeber 28–October 13

Pronunciation: *geh-bo*

Galdr: *ggg-geh-geb*

Gebo (lit. "gift"): Partnership. Everyone wants Gebo in her runecast, not just because it indicates endowments but also because the act of giving has formed a bond. It is not so much about what is received or given, rather its emphasis is on the exchange: something for something.

The idea of a gift for a gift offers lovely promise of good things to come. However, its subtler caveat of a gift given freely indicates a need to give without expectation of receiving. Despite all hints of balanced sacrifice, one should give from the spirit of giving.

Nearing the end of the first ætt, Gebo finds us still in that amorphous space in which we're finding our way into form, into living in the present. Then it happens—we find friends. Through our ability to give to others and receive from them, we create our web—the network of support closest to us, which helps us stay actively involved with All Things. In the Jungian hero's journey this stage is the acquisition of allies, those in form, those in spirit, and those within.

The emphasis on that bond is why Gebo is often associated with partnership. The process of drawing to us those who can truly move us along our paths is a powerful thing. Celtic traditions have the concept of *anam cara,* or "soul friend." Anam cara has most often been mis-interpreted as "soul mate," as in a romantic partner. In reality it speaks to a much higher bond in which each always urges the other toward growth, which bond could be found with a lover, an animal familiar, a place, a child. As we all know, sometimes growth means periods of dis-comfort, and all soul relationships aren't necessarily cheerful. They all, however, hone our sense of self and what we give to the world. The way we learn what we have to give is through sacrifice, through acceptance.

The bottom line when Gebo appears is that someone is coming or will soon come who can help us reach the next significant place of growth. Perhaps both individuals are helped in the joining, perhaps not.

The emphasis is on recognizing that a bond has been made and a new level of self has been attained as a result.

Perhaps best of all, Gebo can't be reversed.

Its challenge is to accept and give freely.

Wunjo

Stave symbol: ᚹ

Half-month dates: October 13–October 28

Pronunciation: *WOON-yoh*

Galdr: *wu-wun-woo-woon*

Wunjo (lit. "joy"): Manifestation. Years ago one of my shamanic teachers told me that he hated moments of clarity. He went on to say that they were wonderful, vivid, heart affirming, though elusive and ultimately not as clear as his ecstasy presented them to be. I knew what he meant, but I remained hopeful that wonder could sustain, that wisdom could override impulse, that awareness could last. He said that clarity always preceded a big fall, and he'd grown to despise the feeling of elements aligning.

I can't say that I share his angst in realizing awareness or any other good thing when it visits, though I fully understand such moments to be delicate and fleeting. This is the message of Wunjo: joy is visiting. Savor it with absolute delight. In this moment alignment with All Things delivers the object of dreams, fruits of labor—clarity. If the moment is a cake glowing with candles, Wunjo is the wish made behind closed eyes. It is the split second during which every cell conspires in support of a deepest desire, and aligned elements usher that manifestation forward.

When Wunjo comes the clarity is real. It is the result of a lot of hard work and being true to one's self. In modern terminology it can be considered all elements of the law of attraction implemented and manifest. Likewise it is our responsibility to locate joy in that outcome. It may come to us unannounced, though we have to be able to recognize it.

The reality is that Wunjo is the end of a cycle—literally the last rune of the first ætt. It's a transient state we pass through when we succeed, complete a trial, then step in to new personhood. The completion of one passage leads to another. That's the story of humanity. The end of a cycle gives us the opportunity to pause, reflect, and derive meaning before we move on to the next challenge. It's our choice to fret what comes next or draw on experience to grow beyond it. Wunjo gives us the option of staying pleasant despite circumstance.

For the record, clarity does last—until with further experience it yields to some other insight.

Joy lasts in memory, it thrives in sharing.

The challenge of Wunjo is to feel joy.

Reversed

When Wunjo visits upended, when joy is tilted, crisis is at hand. Often we think of sadness as the absence of joy; however this stave offers another perspective. As it is the last rune of the first ætt, it symbolizes initiation from one state of being to the next. As the first ætt deals with how we as souls in form bring things into being, it is primarily concerned with how we bring ourselves into being. When we encounter Wunjo reversed, we encounter disappointment with how we are creating ourselves or with some facet of our being.

Most of us have more coping skills for sadness than we do disappointment. In sadness we can surrender to the emotional state of loss, perhaps even grief, and through the introspection it brings we find catharsis beyond it. Disappointment comprises sadness, though it also presents a deeper layer. Because we feel responsible for the failed outcome, we're more likely not to deal with our sadness. We didn't do our best. We didn't honor our intuition. We didn't fulfill a deep need for ourselves. Because we feel responsible for disappointment, we are more likely to deny it, to ignore how let down we feel.

Disappointment in a task, competition, or even our job is one thing. When we view it from the level of Wunjo we're talking about colossal distress over some aspect of ourselves or our lives not being in line with our soul's needs, which when denied becomes at minimum shame and at worst unchecked, long-term, seething rage.

Ever optimistic, Wunjo reversed doesn't just indicate this as the current state of things. It also presents the time frame that is right to confront the source of that letdown. No, we won't suddenly manifest the outcome we wanted, though in seeing the source of the rage or shame for what it is we open our imagination to create a way out of it, which puts us closer to knowing our soul's needs and thus actually meeting them.

SECOND ÆTT

Having learned to nurture and sustain ourselves, we venture into experiencing ourselves among others on their paths doing the same as us. In this ætt we find our divinity among the rubble of everyday human life and learn to sustain it. The second ætt presents our personal rat race alongside others in their own, the tension that parallel creates, and how we deal with it.

Hagalaz

Stave symbol: ᚺ
Half-month dates: October 28–November 13
Pronunciation: *HAHG-ahl-ahz*
Galdr: *ha-hag-al*

Hagalaz (lit. "hail"): Destructive force. This first rune of the second ætt tells an interesting story. Having found a sense of empowered self in the first ætt, we're now challenged to reach beyond ourselves. When this stave presents in a spread, we've finished what we were working on and change is coming. Whether it's the one we've wanted or the one we need is in the eye of the beholder. Regarding runes of change, where Kenaz is the internal inspiring flame, wintry Hagalaz is unexpected external upheaval.

Generally speaking, when we think of hail we don't just shiver and get a little jittery. As hail represents damage, uncontrollable conditions, and extreme cold, we are reminded of water's power to destroy. We must acknowledge its ability to reshape landscapes, social systems, needs, lives. For that reason this first of three winter runes evokes tension.

Likewise we must realize the strength in hail's ability to melt, become usable, or possibly vanish back into nothing. For that reason, and because its shape appears as Uruz perched atop itself in reverse (primal forces opposed), hail is considered not just between states but capable of transmuting itself. Where Uruz is primal states, Hagalaz is primal states in opposition, because it's comprised of Uruz characters pointing away from each other. Because they point away from each other, neither is fully realized and are between states. Seen in this way, Hagalaz presents a universal process through which we all must go—a sort of matrix. It is the first place in the ættir that we greet conflict in form and are forced to draw on our lessons with the first ætt to sustain ourselves as we pass through it. Hagalaz follows Wunjo. The hardest thing about joy is sustaining the memory of it through hard times—especially unexpected hard times.

Because of the dual nature of hail, Hagalaz speaks of betwixt and between states, neither here nor there. With it we begin to distinguish the personal journey from the collective. We begin to clear out dysfunction and move toward what works.

When Hagalaz presents in a spread it doesn't mean that the Multiverse is against us. In fact, it's a reminder to move with the flow, greeting change instead of fighting it. When we realize that hail eventually has to melt, adversity eventually gives way to collaboration, we master the abrupt life force of Hagalaz as the water of melted hail combines with other elements to create growth from destruction. Holding that awareness while embodying some shred of joy is icing (pun intended).

We can't fight the weather. The path of devastation reveals only what stood in its way, what could not bend. Flexibility plods along, pushed to limits perhaps, but unscathed.

This rune cannot be reversed.

The challenge of Hagalaz isn't the change itself but how well we deal with it.

Nauthiz

Stave symbol: ᚾ
Half-month dates: November 13–November 28
Pronunciation: *now-theez*
Galdr: *nau-nah-nauth*

Nauthiz (lit. "need"): Necessity. Anytime this rune comes up, it's appropriate to examine where we're standing in our own way. Interpreted commonly as "need," Nauthiz provokes thoughts of what holds us back, of annoyances we complain about and fret over yet cling to for some unconscious reason. This stave calls upon the angst that lies between choices. The distress isn't about making a choice so much as experiencing the process that reveals it as necessary. What we say we don't want is often the one thing we refuse to change. In that light this rune becomes more about constraint. When Nauthiz appears it indicates that something about our current plan isn't right action; thus now isn't the time to move forward.

This second of the winter runes signals feelings of discontent about something as well as the deep desire to change it. In other words, there is an unmet need. We can't move forward until the need is met. We can't meet the need unless we can identify it.

Related to the youngest of the Norns, Skuld, who is the keeper of what "should" be, this stave is often interpreted as an omen for the future. However wordsmiths among us recognize *should* as a modal auxiliary, indicating that outcomes manifest based on conditions met. In other words, we can set the dominoes up any way we like, and based on our knowledge, skill, and perhaps wisdom, they *should* fall the way we've planned. Yet there are always variables we can't foresee. The dominoes will fall the way they fall, and we have only to react the best way that we can.

Often what we think we *need* is connected to what we think *should* happen, what we *should* get. The appearance of Nauthiz isn't suggesting that we will or won't meet our need but that we be positively certain we can handle what comes. By that I mean that this rune carries the ability to assist us in finding peace, regardless. The gifts it offers are support, patience, and persistence.

It's all connected: identify the need, meet it, move forward; momentum sustained is progress made.

Nauthiz comes down to basic economics. Humans are built to want more, whether it's consciousness, money, or ice cream. Sooner or later we all must learn that there's a balance between what we have, what we want, and how what we will do to get what we want affects us. We must first find that balance within ourselves, then realize there is a greater ledger of balance when it comes to All Things. Nauthiz is the scale upon which we weigh what we think we want and the effort it will take to get it against what we really want and can heartily enjoy having.

This rune has no reversed position.

The challenge of Nauthiz is to consider what needs are filled by not changing.

Isa

Stave symbol: |

Half-month dates: November 28–December 13

Pronunciation: *EE-sah*

Galdr: *i-i-i-i-is-ees-isah*

Isa (lit. "ice"): Stillness. The last of the winter trio, Isa encourages us to be comfortable where we are, because for now, we're not moving. We all have our limits through which we cannot pass until we find the momentum to do so from our deepest reserves. Isa comes when it's time to examine those depths.

Whatever is occurring when this stave is drawn must be dealt with, not just for the pragmatic benefits of doing so but because what comes after cannot manifest until present enlightenment is found. "Enlightenment" sounds dramatic, but that's exactly what is being called for. It's time to push our boundaries, to go beyond what we think we're capable of and what's possible to expect from the world around us.

Perhaps the need is to merely sit and reflect on what needs attention, or it's to acknowledge something long skirting the edge of awareness. Whatever it is, we all recognize that gut-gnawing sensation that says what sustains us is no longer working, that it is hungry for what authentically feeds.

When this stave appears, don't expect to advance. Find a way to engage the stillness. This is the inner spotlight. This is a staycation of the soul. Be uncomfortable where we are, because discomfort motivates change.

The kind of change hinted at with Isa is primal. This stave is often linked to Ymir, the frost giant progenitor of creation. In the Old Norse tradition ice holds the spark of all life—the sacred seed. Associated with the world of Niflheimr, Isa represents the meeting point of the cold yeasty venom, or rime, rivers of Norse mythology flowing from the ice world into heat. This intersection of hot and cold created life. In a sense Isa is associated with self-pregnancy, with abiogenesis. It is a combustion of force and form, such that an entirely new being is created. It prompts the question, "Who will you be?"

This rune can't be reversed. None of the winter runes—Hagalaz, Nauthiz, or Isa—can be reversed. Frozen, indeed.

The challenge of Isa is active rest.

Jera

Stave symbol: ◇

Half-month dates: December 13–December 28

Pronunciation: *YAIR-ah*

Galdr: *yer-yera*

Jera (lit. "year"): Harvest. Many rune enthusiasts view Jera as "year" in the understanding of the sun cycle—dreaming, planting, cultivating, reaping, benefiting, giving, dreaming again. When Jera comes up in a cast the emphasis of that cycle is the harvest, or as I call it, "hearth accounting." In short, finally there's payoff! Jera comes at the time that we have reaped the benefits of hard work and find ourselves in a position to make choices in how we move forward with abundance and awareness.

To evenly maintain ourselves, at the end of harvest there are certain acts in which we should engage. Determine what methods worked and which ones didn't. Decide what new tactics to take. Set aside the portion of the harvest needed to feed us for the next year, what must be reinvested to plant for the next season, and what can be shared with others. The emphasis here isn't extra helpings of bounty, though it's okay to enjoy rewards. Harvest is the time for accumulation of tools, energy, and wisdom that will help us plot and create the next year.

Be realistic. Jera isn't about pie-in-the-sky expenditures or fist-clenching conservation. It indicates the time to truly and deeply assess where we are on every level of being. This stave encourages us to celebrate our accomplishments and then ground ourselves in the plans of what we most want to grow next. In that way we're not just reacting to a cycle; rather we become an active participant in its process.

Given all of that busyness, Jera is walk-don't-run energy. It signifies having come through a major transformation so that finally we are allowed to enjoy the good things it gifted us. This isn't the time to sink into frivolity or drop the momentum. One of the hardest things to do after success is to sustain the pace—neither speed up nor slow down. Hold steady.

Jera is the time for gentle movement and radical self-honesty. It tells us to reward and preserve ourselves and to keep dreaming.

Jera cannot be reversed.

The challenge of Jera is to be accountable to our own process.

Eihwaz

Stave symbol: √↑
Half-month dates: December 28–January 13
Pronunciation: *ay-haz*
Galdr: *eih-eihwa*

Eihwaz (lit. "yew"): Death. Eihwaz is the thirteenth rune. This stave traditionally indicates death. It arrives at the end of something, heralding transformation. The shift that is demanded is into the True Self. This rune implies a corner that must be turned. Life has navigated us such that we can't go back; we can only go forward. Yet the way is blocked by a corner we can't see around. The element of not knowing what comes next is strong with this rune, which is in part why it's associated with death. It presents a terrible tension. In that same sense, "not knowing" can also be equated to faith.

Freya Aswynn connected this rune's tree origins to the Yggdrasil, then to the chakra system.[1] Historically, it's referenced as a yew tree. Because it's poisonous, the yew was often used to make arrows for defense. When thought of as the bridge spanning enlightenment or death, it truly is the medicine that, if poorly held, can kill. I see that connection through the stave's implications of ordeal. Odin scaled and hung from Yggdrasil to learn the mysteries of the Multiverse—the runes. When we read about Odin's ordeal, it's always in a neat, tidy sentence: "Odin hung from the World Tree for nine days and learned the runes." But what does this really say about what he went through and what he did? What does it convey about his experience? Maybe it was horrific. Maybe it was fantastic. Likely it was both.

Extreme experiences of the body engaged in to alter the mind, known as the path of ordeal, have an important place in the study of the runes. In Western culture we don't talk much about sacrifice for self-truth, but when have we ever made a huge stride without ordeal? With the association of Eihwaz as the chakra system, the poisonous yew, and Odin's assertion in the *Elder Edda* that he sacrificed himself to himself, a new light is shed on ordeal and life force awakening. The ordeal Odin experienced didn't just happen to him. He sought it out. He created it, and through that trauma he allowed himself to be altered forever. What he changed in himself brought the runes into human consciousness. He initiated himself into deeper wisdom so that he could serve his community.

The thought of suffering—self-created suffering, no less—to gain awareness leaves most of us cringing. Yet many of us are in the throes of an ordeal without giving it the credit of being what it is. Eihwaz visits with initiation and dictates that we see it through to the finish. Unfinished initiation is crisis—PTSD, to be more precise. When initiation isn't completed, the True Self isn't engaged; thus its wisdom can't be brought forward into community. The message is: realize what burden is carried, let it go, and move on.

With Eihwaz we cannot see our True Selves and remain the same. The emphasis of this stave is on continuity. It demands that we identify what we most need and sacrifice what we must to make sure that we have it, to ensure that we become it. Eihwaz is the mirror image of the self we can't look directly into yet is the self we crave contact with most deeply. Through Eihwaz we learn that we aren't our extremes but rather some balanced place between, some point of power we want to attain without realizing we're already its center.

We can't stay in the World Tree. We can't stay in ecstasy. The whole point of the journey isn't the glory of experiencing the tree but bringing the experience back home, to be lived in the everyday. Eihwaz is truly a "get off the cross, we need the wood" kind of transformation.

Eihwaz can't be reversed.

Its challenge is to greet the True Self and stand in it, ongoing.

Perthro

Stave symbol: ᛈ
Half-month dates: January 13–January 28
Pronunciation: *PER-throw* or *per-drow*
Galdr: *per-perth*

Perthro (lit. meaning unknown): Chance or opportunity. There's no solid consensus on exactly what this rune means. Interpretations running the gamut from "luck" or "gamble" to "karma" abound, though I find that our modern definitions of luck and karma don't come close to describing Perthro's meaning.

Most often discussion of luck sees it as a random force that may work to our advantage or send us packing. However, an older understanding of luck falls more along the lines of a system, a force that ebbs and flows, and our ability to be in touch with that system and know how to read and flow with it determine our success or failure. With that force in mind, Perthro comes to mean more along the lines of "chance" or "opportunity."

Likewise the term *karma* in the West has become plastic, or fake, and generalized. It's been distilled to references such as "good karma" or "bad karma," when in reality it refers merely to balance. There's no basis for reward or punishment, positive or negative. None of us know what balance in any situation may be, so again, we have a strong component of chance.

Imagine a six-sided die. We all know what the potential outcomes of rolling the die are. We know there will be an outcome situated within set criteria—one of six sides. Despite knowing that criteria we still don't know which side will be the outcome. Such is the complexity and simplicity of Perthro.

With every potential for gain, our job is to know our limitations as impeccably as we know our strengths. In that light, Perthro speaks of risk, control, and time—all variables with which the human ego struggles. For that reason, we bring our attention to the process.

Thorsson describes the machinations of Perthro well, commenting on the role of the Norns in its traditional interpretation.[2] The Norns are sisters who keep the Well of Wyrd. Sister Urdhr is what *has* become; Verdhandi, what *is* becoming; and Skuld, what *should* become. Where örlög is primal law or divine order, wyrd is how we interact with it. The Norns represent how we perceive cause and effect in our lives, for how we relate to the process is also the tool by which we accomplish it. The fact that we can examine past actions, plan every little detail, yet still not know how things will turn out—though be assured that they *will* turn out some way—is the emphasis. Perthro's purpose is to make us question, to offer the affirmation of control over the events of our lives, yet remind us there are also other forces at work over which we have no control. These forces can include the deeds of ourselves, our ancestors, our neighbors, our socioeconomic system, our unconscious urges, the positions of the stars.

For many rune enthusiasts Perthro acts as the modern blank rune, bringing to light the unknown, the unknowable. Given these glimpses of its qualities of risk, control, and time, it's easy to see how this stave eludes us still. When I pull it in a reading, the words it speaks to me are, "What do you think?" mirroring my own questions, my wisdom. No, it isn't the magickal answer pulled from the mystery of the Multiverse—or is it? This rune reminds us that we do know the answers to our own questions. However defined, Perthro challenges us to realize that we have as much control as we do not. What is before us now is the change that is always the same. The riddle we constantly mine for meaning and outcome is the truth we're never sure we know.

Ultimately Perthro isn't about setups or outcomes but rather the feelings that arise around what we want, what we perceive we don't have. Its message is to realize that those feelings are actionable, as is—and was—the sacred seed thoughtform.

The challenge of Perthro is to identify success in any outcome.

Reversed

Reversed, Perthro brings a hyper-distilled examination of the moment. That's all we ever have, really, though when Perthro is on the horizon, to live otherwise is to scatter ourselves to the wind. Don't act rashly. No looking forward to what we can't know, no looking back at what is no longer. Be here now.

Expect the unexpected. The second verse is not the same as the first, and we don't necessarily know how this tune will end.

With this upheaved rune comes the whisper that what determines luck isn't the outcome of our efforts but instead how we react to challenge, to the outcome. Owning failure as compassionately as we hold success is how we create luck for later endeavors.

Algiz

Stave symbol: Y
Half-month dates: January 28–February 12
Pronunciation: *ahl-heez* or *ahl-yeez*
Galdr: *ahllaz-ahlyeez*

Algiz (lit. "elk" or "elk-sedge"): Protection. The literal meaning of Algiz is diverse, based on varied interpretations of the rune poems. In its early Germanic uses it indicated elk or stag, though the later Anglo-Saxon poem refers to it as a very sharp grass known as elk-sedge. However interpreted, its protective power remains uncontested.

A deep shape-shifting element makes up this rune, as does masculine Green Man energy. The Nature allies of this stave present strength in spaces indigenous to us, and by knowing the home space so well it gives us the ability to ally so deeply with it that we disappear in it, or shape-shift into it. Herein lies the protection of this stave: we know our strengths. We become them so intensely that we carry them with us wherever we go. For that reason I might argue that this rune carries androgynous elements in that it equally draws upon action (masculine) and embodiment (feminine).

Regardless of how protected we are with Algiz, there is no allowance for resting on our laurels. The stave is also akin to that of a splayed hand, indicating "stay back." We have to know our boundaries and how to enforce them.

Many of us have a hard time creating and enforcing boundaries. However, if we can't do that for ourselves, how can we expect anyone else to stand up for us—divine or mundane? In reality, when we can stand on our own boundaries we are divinely aligned. We are empowered.

When this stave appears in a cast, now is the time to enforce boundaries. Say no, draw the line, and stand on it, knowing the Multiverse stands with us.

The challenge of Algiz is to be the boundary and the one enforcing it.

Reversed

Inverted, Algiz demands that we tend to our limitations. It hints at life areas in which we are vulnerable or not grounded. Likewise it can indicate a time that we feel attacked, attack others unprovoked, or that we can't distinguish our burdens from those of people close to us.

Sowilo

Stave symbol: ζ
Half-month dates: February 12–27
Pronunciation: *so-wih-lo* or *so-wih-lu*
Galdr: *so-su-sol-sul*

Sowilo (lit. "sun"): Divinity/Sacred Power. The presence of Sowilo (or Sowilu) indicates having persevered through hardship and truly mastered the work. Whatever has been pressing, its breakthrough and recently revealed wisdom are lasting. The sun rises to provide us energy, to illuminate clarity. This final rune of the second ætt tells us we can accept this eureka moment as real and enjoy the reprieve that follows.

Anytime Sowilo shows up take the time to celebrate current victory and to revel in the moments of quiet time. Be fully present in looking back at hard work, blessing it, and owning the process that led to this culmination, then proceed with the ability to see self and that experience in a completely different light.

Enjoy, though be attentive to the possibility of overdoing revelry. We rest to honor and heal from what we have toiled to accomplish so that we can be ready to move forward implementing that wisdom. Sunrise indicates time to get up, to become active again. Rest has its place, then we must get on with the day.

There is another, deeper message behind Sowilo. Growing up, I was told in American history classes of how Europeans encountered Native Americans making offerings to the sun and as a result thought they were worshipping it. Early colonists found such rituals profane and blasphemous, contemptuous perspectives that colored their every engagement with the indigenous people of North America.

Many years later I encountered a Sioux man who set that dynamic right. He said that when his people showed gratitude for the sun they were not worshipping the sun. They were celebrating the source behind it, thus the Source behind All Things.

Indeed, this rune reminds us not just of the sun but of the divine power beyond it. As we marvel at the sun's abilities to inspire life on Earth we draw light from it so that we can shine on others. Such is the pay-it-forward connection of All Things, as well as our collective purpose. In this way Sowilo makes the unconscious conscious. We become not just something that divinity happens to, but through. In that interconnection, once we become aware of it, our place isn't to remain passive in that knowledge; rather we are called to act on it.

With this stave think of the way that cats can locate the smallest patch of sunlight, curl themselves to fit it almost precisely, and extract its every second of warmth for the coziest of naps. Sowilo offers a safe, snug ray of light to rest on, for now. Yet even sunlight moves on.

Regardless of where we are in the world, the sun sees us. We're not alone. In realizing that fact, we can't unsee where the sun shines. We are called to act upon its revelations. This calling isn't a possibility but instead a duty.

Sowilo doesn't have a reversed position.

Its challenge is to remind us we are an active part of All Things. We are not just part of but also have the ability to shape our wryd, the tapestry being woven by the Norns with threads that are both personal and collective, the two impacting each other.

THIRD ÆTT

It goes without saying that as the futhark concludes with the third ætt, so do many cycles that play out across the futhark. It also bears observing that while this ætt brings conclusions, it also sets up the recursive nature of the Elder Futhark so that it can all begin again.

The historical references evident in the third ætt play great roles in how the runes of this ætt interact with each other and in the meaning they can bring to our lives. This ætt begins with battle references, traces through a survival story of humanity, and closes with insight on what we can do with that information. In this final ætt we realize our sacred authority.

Tiwaz

Stave symbol: ↑
Half-month dates: February 27–March 14
Pronunciation: *TEE-wahz*
Galdr: *tee-tii-tiir tee-wah*

Tiwaz (lit., the god Týr/Tuisto): Personal Sacrifice. Maybe more than any other rune, Tiwaz speaks of final hurrahs, the eleventh hour, and all the emotions that come with pulling our dreams out of the fire. In short, it depicts having survived the trauma of voluntary sacrifice then having thrived beyond the wound. A phrase I learned in conjunction with this stave is "the battle cry that awakens the second wind." For that reason I call it the survivor rune, and it has direct connections to many of the third ætt staves.

Connected to Týr, the Old Norse war god who sacrificed his hand to the fiendish wolf Fenrir to stave off Ragnarok, this rune is also connected with the lesser-known Germanic god Tuisto. Recall that Tiwaz/Týr/Ymir/Buri is considered the first god in the Old Norse culture. When pressed to survive challenging times, Tuisto created through his son Borr (also called Mannus, represented by the rune Mannaz) another iteration of the human race. Borr was the next iteration of that god procession. When his turn for upset came it seems that Borr struggled with being replaced. He had to lose his position, which also meant losing the people he had loved and led. However, he could let them go, because ultimately he realized that he had the ability through his three sons, Odin, Thor, and Freyr, to sustain humanity. From this adaptation came new peoples, who were the ancient Germanic tribes: Ingaevones (Ingwaz, early word for Freyr), who lived northeast, near the ocean; Herminones (associated with Thor), who lived in the regional center; and the Istavones, who lived along the Rhine River."[3] Likewise Borr's three sons were also known as Véi, Vílir, Vodin, the modern faces of Odin, who eventually were encapsulated into one god—Odin.

These depictions of sacrifice in the name of advancement and adaptation carry deep connotations of serving the greater good, specifically within the realization that the current trajectory will not serve. It cannot, and the only way to right the direction is to sacrifice something dear. That cherished thing is, of course, our heart's song, and, collective good or no, the grief of that realization is almost too much to bear. However it's precisely what carries our new direction—our second wind.

The snag with Tiwaz isn't that we won't get what we want. It's dealing with the ego and emotions regarding not getting it *the way* we want it. I don't say "second wind" lightly. The fevered inhalation Tiwaz presents is the one that comes right before the primal scream—the soul wail for everything we want to create right now but can't, and the grief that comes from that realization.

The underlying force of Tiwaz is that Plan A *will not* work, and getting out of it will not be neat or graceful. Stop trying to force it. Have the tantrum. Make the sacrifice. Grieve the loss, and *let it go*. Step in to courage.

The etheric fuel built up from this inhalation feeds the battle cry that allows the new direction to come. Whatever brainstorm lights through, go with it, because that's the one that's going to change circumstance and return power, enlightenment, inspiration—whatever is needed. The process of letting go of Plan A is what allows Plan B to emerge and root. Tiwaz means that Plan B is the one.

With Tiwaz there is no thinking out of the box. There is no box. Believing that there is one is what we sacrifice. The rote path will not lead to contentment. If it's not a hell yes, it's a hell no.

The message here is that from dire straits amazing outcomes are born, new consciousness emerges. This rune is about realizing that best-laid plans and heart's desires just aren't going to be and then pulling it all out of the fire at the last second with fantastic victory.

The challenge of Tiwaz is finding courage.

Reversed

Consider where ego is preempting the fulfillment of the heart's desire. Reversed, Tiwaz suggests that we've made the sacrifice; however we're not moving on. It encourages us to be honest about reasons for not stepping in to leadership positions. Be attentive to life areas rife with avoidance.

Berkano

Stave symbol: ᛒ
Half-month dates: March 14–March 30
Pronunciation: *behrr-kahn-oh* or *behr-kahn-ah*
Galdr: *bah burk bark berk birk bork*

Berkano (lit. "tree"): Nurture. As with several runes, there are discrepancies about Berkano's specific meaning. Accepted as meaning "birch tree" in the Old Icelandic poem, in the Anglo-Saxon poem it also has been linked to the poplar tree. The Old Norse poem reflects on it as a fir tree. For that reason I present it as "tree." With all these trees in the mix, how do we cull what the forest is telling us about Berkano?

Trees sustain themselves through intense hardship, thus they are attributed with symbolism of the life cycle of birth, chaos, death, and rebirth. All sources note Berkano as a feminine, if not goddess, rune with deep qualities of healing, fertility, and midwifery.

The latter of those I find most telling. Berkano is often demoted to a "mama" rune, though I call shenanigans on that. Mothers, especially new ones, are terrible at emotionally detaching from their children. Everything in them is wired to the tending, protection, and expansion of that kid. In shamanic cultures, past a certain age mothers aren't the soul caretakers of their children, not because they can't do it but because they *shouldn't* do it. They have to let go and let the child find its own way, a process that begins even at birth. For that reason, with Berkano, the emphasis is on the midwife rather than on the mom. This stave calls for an elegant detachment from the event, dynamic, or experience such that it can be facilitated to some closure. This significant distinction between mother and midwife is the crux of the kind of nurturing driving Berkano.

Considering that it follows the heart-wrenching ordeal of Tiwaz, this stave encourages us to grow. It embodies the idea that while the outcome of a project or undertaking may be exactly what we set out to do, by its end we ourselves are not who we thought we were or who we thought we would be. During such progressions we *out*grow things. Our desires and needs change. Perhaps more than either of those, our perspective changes. With the completion of the Tiwaz initiation Berkano sets us up for the healing that must follow, as well as the birthing of our wisdom from ordeal to community.*

In that light there is a trickster element to this rune, as it deals with primal chaos, which alters the manifestation process as we grow with it, as it becomes. While Berkano brings the healing, nurturing, and alliances to deliver what we've created, we may not still want it in the

---

*Ordeal is a specific rite of passage in the Northern Tradition involving subjugation of the body for spiritual evolution. It is our duty to bear the growth/wisdom that comes from ordeal to our community. Ordeal itself is a self-inflicted painful revelation of wisdom that was so hard-won that you have to do something with it to justify the difficulty of gaining it. The healing process that leads to bearing that wisdom to the betterment of community is a component of Berkano.

end. This connection is another link to the evergreen fir tree via Loki's mother, Laufey.

Carrying the message of "dues paid," with Berkano we can begin again. When it visits, truly potent outcomes are brewing. Stay with the process of their development and carefully tend their needs, as well as personal ones. We have gestated, and what can be born from that is on its way or has just occurred.

Berkano urges us to realize what we really want and to set every aspect of our lives with that desire. We can't do that by looking back at what we could have or should have done, or by projecting into what the next big project should be. Berkano demands that we be in the moment and celebrate it. In doing so we align with our True Self.

Berkano challenges us to heal.

Reversed

This stave reversed indicates where we are not authentically identifying or engaging in our creative process. It may be writer's block, collaborative efforts falling apart, or a time to focus on what is rather than what can be.

Ehwaz

Stave symbol: ᛗ
Half-month dates: March 30–April 14
Pronunciation: *EH-wahz*
Galdr: *ehhh-ehwah*

Ehwaz (lit. "horse"): Momentum. Found only in the Germanic and Anglo systems, Ehwaz is an interesting rune. Simply put, the horse provides transportation to take us from one place to another. Traveling great distances and over challenging terrain, it allows us to accomplish what would ordinarily be beyond our human capabilities. The horse works for us, yet despite domestication maintains a wildness of spirit that humanity admires and can never touch. Because of that the horse bestows power upon humans. It gives us cooperative teamwork by providing strength greater than our own and provokes questions of our own domestication. It gives us momentum.

In Old Norse mythology the horse was humanity's *fylgja,* or "fetch," one who leads us to wisdom, a journey that doesn't equate to "joy ride." This totemic image becomes particularly significant coupled with that of Sleipner, Odin's eight-legged horse who carried him to traverse the realms of Yggdrasil, from which he gained insight into the runes. This movement between worlds brings the torment of enlightenment, followed by the inability to return to everyday life as the same person. With Ehwaz we again brush against the tension of ordeal, a process that harkens back to the traditional shamanic death. The metaphor of traveling from the everyday into an etheric expression of it only to return pressed to heal spiritual crisis is the original healing story, the ouroboros (or Jörmungandr) shamanic narrative that we all participate in, repeatedly.

When Ehwaz appears, initiation is upon us. It brings a piercing of the heart with insight from which we cannot turn away. It embodies moving through experiences that bring us to a more suitable awareness, that which we crave at our deepest levels. This stave portends that our travel on the back of awakening is in the process of depositing us on the doorstep of new wisdom.

Let it be. Don't try to manhandle the reins and control the outcome. This is neither the time to enslave a beast of burden nor to glide obliviously through scenery without being active in the journey. When Ehwaz comes we are being called to be aware and engaged, to see this trip through to the end.

Remember, when the Aztecs and Incas first saw a mounted conquistador they interpreted it as one animal, a kenning along the lines of "two-headed centaur."[4] While we know the miraculous technology of riding horseback comprises human and horse, let's not forget the animistic bond of seeker and Nature ally. We're not alone, and we're not without guidance.

The challenge of Ehwaz is to sustain momentum.

Reversed

Ehwaz reversed evokes feelings of being lost, offtrack, or confused. It indicates where thinking has become unclear, and the scope of a project, relationship, or dynamic has crept from its intention. Evaluate the intention, and if necessary, take a prolonged pit stop until things are back on track.

Mannaz

Stave symbol: ᛗ
Half-month dates: April 14–April 29
Pronunciation: *MAHN-nahz*
Galdr: *mah-mahn-mahna-mahnu*

Mannaz (lit. "human"): Community. Through Tiwaz we had our first glance of Mannaz via Mannus (Borr), the Germanic god who created the three principal human tribes. Mannaz fosters our fullest potential. Relationships are key, and whatever is on the agenda can only be accomplished when we make use of our collective resources. This stave points to success in work and indicates a time of outer and inner balance.

I call Mannaz the animistic rune, though that could likely be said about all of them. I see this stave as Wunjo facing itself. Wunjo is the rune of joy or delight, which some modern practitioners characterize as the law of attraction, or wyrdweaving—the point at which we've figured out that we are creators in our own right and have learned to use the tools that come with the territory of co-creation. This combination makes Mannaz Joy beholding itself. By finding joy where we are, joy finds us everywhere. The effect of Mannaz, in that case, would be how what we create in ourselves affects all around us. What joy we find in ourselves we become capable of finding in all.

From a shamanic standpoint, in cosmologies Mannaz represents the strata where humans are most directly empowered—Midgard, or "middle yard"—Earth middle. It's the place of Earth spirituality, the fae, Nature Spirits, and the pool of our formed wisdom and compassion. From a shamanistic standpoint it exalts the ego and body, which are the focus of "Middle World" work. It is the domain of mind guiding matter.

When Mannaz presents in a cast, it signifies time to get new thoughts on a subject. Specifically, it points to the need to find a new social group that can help cultivate the wisdom processed from the ordeal of Tiwaz. Often when we've come through a radical initiation we emerge so changed that our current communities can't honor what we've experienced. We need new life, new eyes, a new take on things. When we encounter Mannaz it's time to find that new community. It's time for the open mic of the soul.

Just as Mannaz indicates humans interconnected and drawing on the spiritual resources in their home domain, it also illuminates the human being in balance with self. As we draw on the support of those around us so should we truly, deeply support ourselves. This act of self-love is our calling, our gift, and our greatest secret potential. Feeling so deeply connected to self and others brings a "green means go" kind of support, being carried on the shoulders of Mannaz.

The challenge of Mannaz is to recognize community and the role of our communal self.

Reversed
Be aware of feeling disconnected, where perception of the greater flow has been affected. Be careful in connecting with others when this rune appears reversed. Perhaps the way we relate to others isn't as we think, we're resisting finding a new community, or we've become confused in the way we relate to self. Despite that, Mannaz reversed indicates feeling outside the web of All Things, so it portends our rejoining.

Laguz

Stave symbol: ↑
Half-month dates: April 29–May 14
Pronunciation: *lah-GOOZ*
Galdr: *lah-lahgu*

Laguz (lit. "water"): Flow. Laguz is a comfy rune. Watery, feminine, and intuitive, it speaks to our primal imperative to always point home. There is a saying, "water always finds its level," meaning that no matter what storm moves through, how violently water is stirred, or where land dries to drought, water finds its still nature. It will always find its way back to its source. It will always flow to the ocean. With that programmed imperative, when Laguz appears it speaks to matters of returning home.

Symbolically speaking, its inherent ability to adapt is its gift to us. In that light Laguz isn't just about water but also about flow. The mutable, emotional element, Laguz is the realization of abundance, the indicator of All Things flowing as Nature intends. That sounds nice and tidy, though the water element is anything but. When we think of flow most of us envision a stream, a neat current framed by boundaries, picturesque evidence that life goes on regardless of debris in the way. We forget that it can be torrential, smothering, devastating, and overwhelming when its boundaries are overrun. Regardless of how it's contained, the space around water is defined by it. Every stone, shell, grain of sand, blade of grass, animal, perhaps human in its vicinity is shaped by how water moves along its path. In that light water takes care of itself.

Likewise water cannot be forced to go faster or slower. Standing still in flow can leave you overtaken by it. Lazing along its surface, the current can carry you places you didn't intend to go. Working with Laguz requires mindfulness, with finesse.

Associated with the feminine and unconscious drives, anytime this rune comes up in a reading there is an emphasis on honoring the natural pace of things. Sometimes it can be hard to do that, as we keep ourselves artificially busy with work, entertainment, distraction, and so forth. Some of us aren't in touch with our natural rhythms, while others of us are though may not want to go where life is leading us.

The challenge of Laguz is to allow elemental support.

Reversed

The warning not to overreach is the law of Laguz reversed. It calls us to find the places where we're out of joint with the elements, if not outright forcing outcomes. The only reason anyone ever swims against the current is because they feel unsupported by it. We can't heal what we don't feel. Resist fear and the reflex to hold back from what feels right. Examine what is out of sync, and take to heart all options. Go with the flow. We can't make wrong choices. All we can do is continue making the best choices from the options we have available at any moment. The message of Laguz reversed is that we can create change for ourselves, on our own terms, or the Multiverse will make it for us.

Ingwaz

Stave symbol: ◇
Half-month date: May 14–May 29
Pronunciation: *ING-wahz*
Galdr: *iiing-eng*

Ingwaz (lit. "people of Ing"): Birth/Outcome. As the People of Ing, or Ingvaeones, are the progeny of Tuisto, with Ingwaz we reiterate the Tiwaz theme that from dire straits amazing outcomes are born. This stave also carries the caveat that outcomes don't appear as expected. Regardless, it symbolizes that our wisdom prevails over external challenge. It affirms that where there's a will there's a way. Know this part of the journey is drawing to a close, if not finished. The dream is manifesting. The dawn of new mindedness is here.

Ingwaz is what I call a "hinge" rune in that it's about that liminal space—or maybe non-space—swinging between *here* and *there*. It's not so much about the events themselves, where we started, or where we end up; rather it emphasizes how the whole process changed us inside. Ingwaz points to that well of the murky middle area, the inner void where we create ourselves every day and conscientiously intentionally begin that creation process every day. Not the past and not the future, that present middle place is always our greatest seat of power.

Another current of Ingwaz is its relationship to Isa. As working through the entire Elder Futhark is an initiation, embedded rites emerge in the course of the practice. Among them is the process of ice's sacred seed, the state of the suspended thoughtform preparing to burst in to being. Tiwaz brings the point that our sacredness is challenged in some way, externally, which signals the need for internal revolution. Mannaz forces us to take our new awareness out for a spin. We were challenged to bear the results of germinating that sacred seed and moving through the grief of what that means in human terms and show our gooey insides to other people. Having done so Ingwaz represents that bright shiny new consciousness birthed. It is the sacred seed in form. It is the culmination of everything that seed went through, every thought and feeling it had about that process, the receptacle of what everyone else thought about that process, the wounds, scars, strengths, and power of its every step into being.

Drawing on that deep inspiration and quiet reverence, Ingwaz is subtle. Think of this time as the final gestation hours of dreams. The basic framework is in place, born of sacrifice and intense change. Worked muscles must rest. Wounds must mend. Final touches must be glossed on slowly, gently. Knowledge and experience marinate into wisdom. So rest, allow, and in doing so engage deepest truth.

We tend to look for progress as this steady jaunt to some expected outcome, checking completed items off a list along the way. Ingwaz reminds us that true progress is measured not by our ability to reach the finish line first but to reach it in a way that supports and fosters our integrity, shares our truth, and inspires others to hold to theirs.

In short, Ingwaz cautions us that plans change, and it's okay to roll with what comes. In fact, if we find that our plans have changed and kick in the reflex to fight it, then the things we want most can't come into being. No matter what lies ahead, what plans have been made, what desires motivate, all we can really work with is the present.

This stave has no reversed position.

The challenge of Ingwaz is to be present in the new way.

Dagaz

Stave symbol: ⋈
Half-month date: June 14–June 29
Pronunciation: *DAH-gahz*
Galdr: *dah-dahg-dahga*

Dagaz (lit. "day"): Epiphany. The second to last rune, Dagaz is translated as "day," though it means more than just a turn on Earth's axis.

This rune places great emphasis on the sun, on light. In the Old Norse tradition Dagaz indicated Baldur, specifically his murder, as it represented the sun's demise. As such, Summer Solstice is suspended time. It's the day of most sunlight, least darkness.

Because we frame days by essential opposites—twilight to dawn, sunrise to sunset—we forget to be attentive to what happens between these polarities, not just the state of light shifting to darkness or the dark becoming illuminated. We must explore the point at which they are one and the same. Dagaz urges us into the place where those extremes meet. Like that meeting place, we are fully neither or are some combination of both. We are liminal. We are this and that. We are here and there. We are the rock and the hard place. We are the enlightened and enlightenment.

What often gets short shrift in the nuance of this stave is exactly how climactic that conclusion is and the fact that it culminates in the acquisition of long-sought wisdom. Dagaz marks the arrival at the gods, the pinnacle revelation of a pilgrimage having met its intention and concluded on a very high note.

So what does one do after sitting at the feet of the gods? With Tiwaz I wrote about the primal silence that comes before the scream, how little attention is given to what force it carries, what power it takes to draw in the breath to exhale change. We likewise never talk about the deafening silence after, which is where I plot Dagaz. The drama is over, and drama it was. What in the world comes next?

For a lot of us emptiness ensues, and it is easily filled with vapid escapism, anxiety over not being on a hero's journey, or sheer depression that the end wasn't as expected. For this reason I call Dagaz the "So what?" rune. Yes, we've come this far! Yes, we did it! So what? Life doesn't end. It doesn't settle into some quaint closure, then the credits roll. Remember that with the runic calendar Dagaz is the final stave in the ordering. Its ultimate message emphasizes knowing what meaning is required from every day and having a game plan to both manage the quiet that comes at the end and deal with the fact that it will all start all over: a different drama, a new need, a strange journey—twenty-three staves' worth.

Bringing in elements of accountability, this stave draws our awareness to micro-cycles. Where Jera, in the second ætt, speaks of the annual harvest, Dagaz indicates the daily reaping. Representing the close of a full day's work this metaphor for celebrating the culmination of a cycle and regrouping to begin another day is telling.

Like Jera it portends observing the bigger needs—noticing what came in, what went out, what worked, what didn't, what to repeat, what new tricks to implement, what to save, what to throw away, what to give. That's Hearth Accounting 101. Because it focuses on such a slim slice of time, Dagaz is about *heart accounting*. It gives the opportunity to realize what of the day had meaning, with whom we spent our time, what was joyful, where we need more joy, how attitude affects all of the above. Internal auditing is important here.

All told, Dagaz is about transcendence. It indicates that we haven't just gotten through or completed the mundane task. We have integrated its consciousness into our own, internalized its wisdom to some epiphany. This sense of closure encourages us not to get too emotionally involved. Keep the ego in check and do our best, because in the end there is no end. We've reached the mountaintop and are left to—what? Realize that we've done this process before, and we'll do it again, with a promise of good things coming to those who wake.

Because of that recursive feel it's worth noting that some rune scholars posit Dagaz as the last futhark rune, rather than Othala. When working with both of these staves consider their differing emphasis on closure and opening, what we keep and what we pass on.

Dagaz has no reversed position.

The challenge of Dagaz is to become reinspired.

Othala

Stave symbol: ⊗
Half-month date: May 29–June 14
Pronunciation: *oh-thal-ah*
Galdr: *oh-ohd-ohda*

Othala (lit. "inherited property"): Legacy/Ancestors. Othala is the last rune of the three Elder Futhark ættir. While Othala literally translates as "property," its implementation is more along the lines of "that which we inherit and pass on."

Where Fehu concerns wealth that requires tending, is collected, and accounted for, Othala calls our attention to a different kind of prosperity—that which we share, that comes before us, and that will outlast us. Focused on All Things clan, its implications go far beyond being related, pooled resources, and protection in numbers. Certainly these practical matters are important when it comes to the preservation of land, defense of lineage, and assurance of inheritance. To our for-bearers Othala represented a wholly unified spirituality spanning this life to the next and what came before—a community of souls that transcended the corporeal boundaries of time and space. To them the ancestors remained alive and active in death, informants of every facet of clan life. They maintained a voice in the direction of how their descendants carried the line forward. Ancestors were accessible for guidance on practical and spiritual matters.

Likewise Othala brings our thoughts to elderhood. At some point we all become elders, leaders of those who led us, those whom we birthed. It becomes our job to heal old ancestral wounds and not bring them into the present. We are required to stay attuned to the ancestral purpose and make peace with manifesting it authentically yet in congruence with our personal goals.

With this collective experience of being in mind, this stave calls on us to examine the separation between what we know and cherish and what we don't know and fear. The only foundation we can stand on to distinguish such is wisdom, and that foundation is strong and wide. We aren't alone, and in the process of finding how we move forward, remember that as we draw on what came before to support, inform, and sustain us, so do we leave behind a precious and informed trail that others will follow.

Othala encourages us to focus on the value we have created with our time here, on that which will go on long after we're gone. Through it we are faced with legacy, the one we pick up and do our best with, and the one we leave for others to step in to. It tells us to look no further than our own backyard for how we can deepen our connection with All

Things, because if we can't find our connection with All Things in our own backyard, we were never really aware of it to begin with.

Given its portal-like bridge connecting past and future into a distilled present, Othala is associated with Odin. In the Old Norse cosmology he was the father elder as well as our promise of what would come.

The challenge of Othala is to bless our lessons and transmit what we've learned.

Reversed

To live well we must be able to distinguish the pain of our present lives from that of our elders and release both. Othala reversed demands that we behold personal wisdom and find the courage to share it. We must become the elder in our line. When we don't own amassed knowledge and wisdom then we hand down wounds for our children to heal. This is a weight no *one* can bear. Realize personal connection to sacred ancestry and become active in it. Relieve and release it.

4
The Runic Calendar
Structure and Sacred Rites

There are many iterations of runic calendars, which were also called runic calendar "staffs" (because they were often carved into long planks of wood). The timekeeping and presentation of these calendars differ by solar and lunar cycle, region, culture, and era, resulting in what can be called a relative chronology. In fact, so in tune with Nature and stellar cycles were some ancient rune calendars that the placement of staves changed year to year, particularly with regard to weekdays. A common convention began the calendar the first full moon after Winter Solstice, while others sourced the calendar's beginning at the start of summer. These runic calendars predate the Gregorian calendar; thus in their methodology they have little in common with the contemporary calendar. With such wide variety in use over time, interpretations, and regional discrepancies, it's important to keep an open mind regarding the flux of the runic calendar and to drop linear associations retrofitting it precisely to the Gregorian calendar.

The basis of what is accepted now as the runic calendar stems from a distillation of these earlier calendars and lines in the *Völuspá* and *Hávamál* poems. Rune scholar Freya Aswynn postulated that the Nine Worlds correlated with the nine runes that can't be reversed, and the twelve palaces of the Grímnismál with the twelve contemporary zodiac signs.[1] With those associations author Nigel Pennick later deconstructed various seasonal cycles of Germanic, Anglo, and Celtic traditions of northern Europe, honored their overlaps with each other and the runes, and set the calendar's base structure of timekeeping according to the Elder Futhark.[2]

It's a worthy argument. Ultimately these scholars sat down and distilled many runic calendars, the ancient writings, and the cultural flavors of northern regions to create a calendar that would have meaning in modern lives. This reconstructed calendar is the basis of the runic devotions and initiations offered in this text.

If the flow of the calendar as it's laid out in this book doesn't jibe for you, explore others. Based on your geolocation and time zone you can create your own. Regardless of where you live, the devotions and initiations of this book can still be tailored to your geolocation and how you create a direct relationship with the runes.

It's also significant to note that seasonal endings don't immediately roll into a new beginning. There's often a transitional time between the two, which for modern seekers may feel outside the way we prefer to experience linear time. Go with what works for you.

CALENDAR STRUCTURE

For the purposes of this text the runic cycles are noted in the predominant order of the Elder Futhark, with the exception of Dagaz. In this runic calendar Dagaz is the final rune, rather than Othala. Likewise the traditional order of the Elder Futhark begins with Fehu, which for the runic calendar corresponds to June 29.[3] This proximity to Summer Solstice brings the new year in this calendar. Please note that for the Southern Hemisphere the dates in the calendar are flipped—Summer Solstice falls in December and the calendar begins with Fehu on December 28 and proceeds from there.

There are twenty-four half-months, with a rune assigned to each, in sequence. Each half-month correlates to one twenty-fourth of the solar year cycle, which is roughly fifteen and a quarter days, the historic "fortnight."[4] Each rune moves in to the focus at different times of day, as noted in the list on page 72 (times are local apparent). Each day has a stave, as does each hour. With this information it's possible to correlate life events—such as births and deaths—with their presiding runes; thus it's possible to understand the wyrd qualities of such events by interpreting their runes.

The Runic Half-Months

Fehu: June 29 (3 a.m.)–July 14

Uruz: July 14 (8 a.m.)–July 29

Thurisaz: July 29 (2 p.m.)–August 13

Ansuz: August 13 (7 p.m.)–August 29

Raidho: August 29 (12 a.m.)–September 13

Kenaz: September 13 (6 a.m.)–September 28

Gebo: September 28 (11 a.m.)–October 13

Wunjo: October 13 (4 p.m.)–October 28

Hagalaz: October 28 (10 p.m.)–November 13

Nauthiz: November 13 (3 a.m.)–November 28

Isa: November 28 (8 a.m.)–December 13

Jera: December 13 (2 p.m.)–December 28

Eihwaz: December 28 (7 p.m.)–January 13

Perthro: January 13 (1 a.m.)–January 28

Algiz: January 28 (5 a.m.)–February 12

Sowilo: February 12 (10 a.m.)–February 27

Tiwaz: February 27 (4 p.m.)–March 14

Berkano: March 14 (9 p.m)–March 30

Ehwaz: March 30 (2 a.m.)–April 14

Mannaz: April 14 (7 a.m.)–April 29

Laguz: April 29 (12 p.m.)–May 14

Ingwaz: May 14 (6 p.m.)–May 29

Othala: May 29 (11 p.m.)–June 14

Dagaz: June 14 (4 a.m.)–June 29

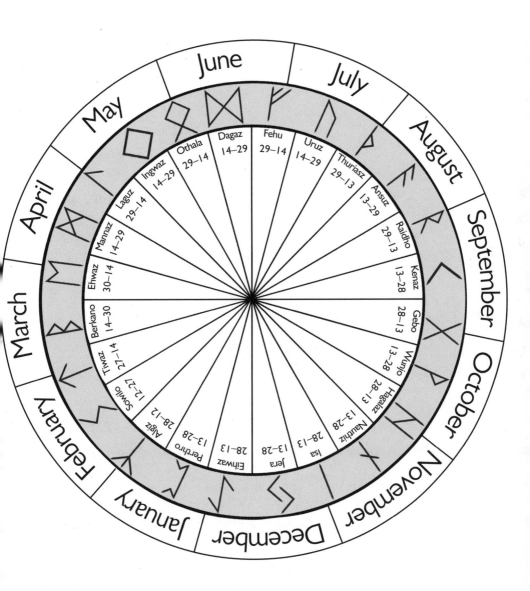

Runic Half-Month Calendar

The half-month's rune indicates the energies most available and the dynamics most in play during the given fortnight. The rune indicates the tone of the season, though you can engage with each time period as you feel led. Ultimately the significance of placement of runes on the wheel of the year lies in personal meaning. If content has meaning for you that's the true test. And not all of the runes or time placements will resonate—that's okay.

One way to connect with the runes is to do rune readings as you progress through this work. Depending on the intention you set for readings they can add nuance and clarification to how to best make use of the half-month strengths, implement the devotionals, and approach sabbat initiations. Along with making notes on the devotionals and sabbat initiations, be prepared to keep a journal alongside this seasonal work. The ability to track patterns over time while observing the shifting influence of the runes heavily affects the meaning this work takes in your life. Being able to look back over events that have played out during specific half-months will help you to see the cycles within the ættir, as well as to note the cycles in the runes unique to you in each year.

THE SABBATS

The eight sabbats make up the Nature holy days honored by many modern pagan traditions. The solstices and equinoxes make up the major sabbats, while the cross-quarter days, or midpoints between the solstices and equinoxes, are celebrated as well.

While observation of the sabbats and what they were called differed across northern European cultures and regions, that holy days were honored as unique moments in the Earth's movement around the sun was consistent. For some modern seekers this logic won't be sound. The cultural divides are too great, and the rituals for honoring Nature's moments are too different from each other. It's okay to question whether seasonal observations of different pockets of ancients— who didn't have the same observations as each other then—can be overlaid on our sense of time, culture, season, and location. In truth I would hope that anyone on a modern path would question the validity of drawing in the sacred rites of a time, place, and culture different from his or her own.

From my perspective this is a concern that all modern pagans must make peace with, as we are not the ancestors. Most of us are no longer in ancestral lands, we don't share common weather patterns (thus precise seasonal focuses), and we can't outright claim sameness of path. Some of us share no common ancestry with the northern lands. Some of us do share an ancestry and sustain a very romanticized idea of what life in ancient times in those locations was like and hold our spiritual path up to that same logic. Given such disparities, are we to put down the runes and reject their insights?

That's up to you. When studying the runes according to time and place we have to ask ourselves, "Do I want to force the remnants of a historic way of looking at the runes as they relate to time and place from the vantage point of one isolated region, which is its own kind of rigid, linear retrofitting, or do I want to create a useful, fluid experience with the runes in the present, based on what we know of the past's wisdom?"

A lot of people interested in studying the runes don't hail from northern Europe. And many who do have origins in northern Europe have no current tie to northern traditions. Yet despite migration, cultural differences, spiritual dispositions, prejudice, even climate change, the sun is where it was. We move around it, like we always have. These scientific and ancestral facts give us enough grounding to strike out with the runes against the backdrop of the sabbat wheel, even if our modern lives and experience of regions don't overlay perfectly those of the Old Norse. You can still honor the runic cycles of the Old Norse path on your land while honoring the Nature Spirits of your region in your own way.

Through the sun's death and rebirth path the runes reveal to us what natural threads of the wyrd are available to us at each sabbat. Call them what you will, as how you speak them deepens their resonance. How we reference sabbats in modern pagan culture isn't the way they were honored in the Old Norse culture. I reference them as we know them now, paying as much homage as possible to the cultural overlaps and distinctions. For the purposes of this book the sabbats include:

+ Summer Solstice/Midsummer/Litha
+ Lughnasadh/Lithasblot/Lammas (the first-harvest holy day)
+ Autumnal Equinox/Mabon (the second-harvest holy day)
+ Samhain (the final-harvest holy day)
+ Yule/Winter Solstice/Midwinter
+ Imbolc/Disting
+ Vernal Equinox/Ostara
+ Beltane/Walpurgisnacht

Coinciding with the Celtic holy day of Beltane, the Old Norse observance of Walpurgisnacht actually spans nine nights and commemorates Odin's ordeal on Yggdrasil. It occurs between April 22 and May 1, which is the period between Ostara and Beltane. Winternacht (Winter Nights) is another observance that factored into the Old Norse calendar. Some cultures place it in mid-October though it is often observed for three days around Samhain. It is characterized by visits with the *dísir* (female ancestor spirits) and remembrance of loved ones past.

This book isn't intended to be a primer on the sabbats. In fact it assumes no specific knowledge about them other than general consensus about them and their observance. This openness is to allow for the fact that we honor these times of the year differently across traditions.

TIMING OF THE SABBATS

It's important to note that contrary to popular belief the sabbats don't occur at the exact same time every year. They can vary by as little as a day and as much as two days. To learn the true timing of sabbats based on local time and location, consult a universal time calculator. Such calculators factor in latitude and longitude as well as corrections for Daylight Saving Time. As the sabbats are focused on drawing down the life force of the stellar alignment, many folks prefer to do their rituals on the calculated dates and times, as the impact of the stars is most powerful then. As well, timing of the sabbats is significant, as the midpoint of the half-month is when the seasonal rune is most powerful. Thus the midpoint of the half-month is the best time to give extra focus to affirmations, galdr, personal devotional work, and sabbat initiations. Ultimately do the work in the timing that best fits your needs and availability.

Also, most of what is celebrated as "traditional sabbat observation" is based on the seasonal progression of the Northern Hemisphere. Today traditions from the northern European region have traveled the globe and have adapted to other seasonal observations. It is possible to adapt the runic calendar to other regions by still following the stave order set forward and basing its progression on local time calculations. The dates indicated in this book are based on the Northern Tradition observation of sabbats.

Honoring the sabbats now is still deeply indicative of seasonal insights for some, though for most it lacks that earth-based awareness. Modern life doesn't require us to be as vigilant to what Nature is doing. We are climate-controlled, likely in locales that track a different seasonal timing, indifferent to the celestial map, and we don't work the land such that we carry a visceral bond with it throughout our days. For many, acknowledging the sabbats is a symbolic gesture not only to the seasonal progression but also to those who came before us, who lived and died by that wheel. Implementing a runic observation of the sabbats maintains the seasonal sentiment and deepens our relationship to its wisdom.

To really bring that observation into direct relationship, get outside with the runes in season. Sing their galdr to the water, air, and land and all the beings that inhabit them. Begin seeking the places where you and the land you live on are the same—shared needs, strengths—so that you can bring that foundation into your runic calendar work. Again, keep a journal of your experiences, not just with each rune but with each season through your immediate observation of where you live.

Regarding the best season to begin the runic devotionals, you can start in any season, with any sabbat. While there are cycle markers for beginning season and flow throughout, Nature is always available. Just go to the chapter associated with your current season, and begin with its work.

This series of devotionals and initiations can be repeated every year. New awareness comes. No two sabbats bring the same insight. No two experiences with the same rune will be the same.

The key allowance in this work is nuance. Read, study, experience, yet stay open through it all to allow it to grow into something beyond what you already know.

DEVOTIONALS

Devotion is a practice often lost to modern pagans. As we don't have a central organizational structure for our faith we are often not well informed about how to create one for ourselves. Originating in the early thirteenth century from the Old French *devocion,* it suggests that devotion is regularly expressed passion toward some spiritual undertaking, as in "the act of dedicating or consecrating by a vow; to sacrifice oneself or promise solemnly."[5]

In short, a devotional is a loosely structured, short regular practice to stay aligned with some spiritual focus. It provides a purpose, format, and dedicated time to focus spiritual awareness. For our use the seasonal sabbat procession provides the purpose and structure for our practice (initiations), while the runic calendar creates the dedicated time (devotionals).

How are devotionals and initiations connected? Balance is not the human norm. Life means repeatedly losing center, it means continuous challenge. Sometimes we get to choose the challenge, sometimes we don't. However, when we have a spiritual foundation based in a regular practice that we are intimately connected to, we cultivate a well from which to draw strength, insight, and momentum. The runic devotionals serve to create this foundation so that when we meet initiations— those sacred ones offered at the sabbats or everyday ones encountered by chance—we can draw from that well and rise to the challenge with confidence.

To make the best use of devotionals, engage with the information about the runes in this part of this book. Work with the runes, regularly, and ideally with ample time for each so that you internalize how each shows up in your life, and you don't overwhelm yourself with new information. I also think that studying the runes is, in itself, is an initiatory experience. Too much too quickly will create stress. Each rune is meant to be slowly ingested to the point where one is ready to move on to the next one.

Working with the runes regularly is the only way you can truly connect with them. Indeed read, study, and verify multiple resources on them. However, reading and study can only get you so far. You must engage them through other senses. Hold them. Feel them. Draw them on your food and eat them. Work with them in casts for yourself. Purposefully put yourself in the place of having conversations about them with others, possibly through doing casts for others. When you can create, sustain, and respond to dialogue about the runes your synaptic connections to them become immediate.

For me the deepest engagement comes when I feel them in my body, which is through galdr. Their resonances and tones tingle through my form, and I feel connected to their source. Also I devote time to call in the spirit of the stave and spend time with each, moving through them in relationship as I progress through the season.

The belief that all things have souls, or spiritual agency, is animism. In that perspective all things can be communicated with (as long as they want to be); thus a direct relationship can be forged. Instead of solely relying on other resources to determine what the runes mean, you can also engage in relationships with the spirits of them, with each ætt, and with the futhark as a whole.

As always, keep a journal. Make detailed notes. Your journal will become the grimoire that sustains your evolution with the Elder Futhark.

INITIATIONS

While devotion may be a less familiar concept to modern pagans, initiation, in theory, isn't. The word originated from the Latin *initiationem,* meaning "participation in secret rites."[6] In its application initiation can mean many things and take many forms.

Modern pagan elder Isaac Bonewits broke the understanding of initiation into three categories: initiation as a recognition of a status already gained, initiation as an ordeal of transformation, and initiation as a method for transferring spiritual knowledge and power.[7] Chances are you will experience each of these types of initiations as you work with the runic calendar. Some will present territory that's familiar and internalized, while others will bring new frontiers with challenges that were unforeseen.

Initiatory cycles exist all through the Elder Futhark. It is my belief that such cycles are part of its magickal purpose. In fact every rune could be considered as having its own initiatory component. As you work through the seasons allow those organic transformations to arise as you also tend the sabbat initiations set forth in this book.

In our study of the runic calendar the eight sabbats on the wheel of the year occur within the half-months, for which the rune of that half-month gives support. Sabbat initiations replace the rune devotionals for those eight half-months. Sabbats are by nature initiations. In particular the solstices challenge our sense of mortality by altering our relationship to light and darkness. The equinoxes confront us with attachments to change, while the cross-quarter holy days keep us on point in our observations of endings and beginnings. Bringing a runic focus to the challenges inherent in the sabbats helps us be better prepared for those times of the year and more thoroughly internalize what those seasons have to teach us.

We see sabbat initiations coming every year, which means we get a chance to do them over again. Through the runic calendar's cycle of devoted study we not only gain ground to re-find center through the wisdom of the runes, we have the opportunity to prepare. The insights we take into the known sabbat initiations leave us better qualified to manage the initiations we don't see coming.

The reality of any initiation is that it's only useful if completed. Beginning an initiation then not completing it generates distress, perhaps even PTSD, and if you're in the shamanic vernacular, soul loss. I say this not to dissuade you from this study of the runic calendar but to fully emphasize the significance of this work. It will change you. It's supposed to change you. Give it the proper context within your life to do so, trust yourself to go where you most need to go with it, and by all means finish what you start.

Whatever challenges you meet in the calendar work, be prepared for how you will cope with the changes these initiations bring to your life. If you're currently in an esoteric mentoring study, or working with someone else to sustain your spiritual, emotional, or psychological well-being, include that person in your plan to incorporate this study of the runic calendar into your personal devotional and initiation studies. It helps to have someone you know and trust to help you process the things that come up in your work. If I can provide support, feel free to contact me through Soul Intent Arts, www.soulintentarts.com.

AFFIRMATIONS

Along with emphasizing galdr as a technique to facilitate coming in to relationship with each half-month rune, each half-month chapter closes with an affirmation. These affirmations capture the story of each rune and make it relatable in the day-to-day. Saying the affirmations aloud helps you learn the story of the runes and to live their cycle.

If I can be of service in helping you connect with the runes feel free to contact me through my website: soulintentarts.com. Also, the *Living the Runic Book of Days* Facebook group is available to those who would like to process their experiences of the book among others who have read it and seek witness as they move through the seasons.

Community makes all the difference on a healing and ecstatic path and can be the most valuable aspect of completing initiation. If for no other purpose than to be witnessed, find and make use of communities that can foster your work with the runic calendar.

PART 2
LIVING THE RUNES

5
June 29–July 14
✦ Fehu ✦
Manifesting the Sacred Self

Fehu comes on the heels of Summer Solstice, midpoint of a season that carries intense energy. Moving from the spotlight of Dagaz to the grounded care of Fehu brings closure and support to what has been a transformational time. Most certainly, shifting from Dagaz to Fehu redirects the focus to more everyday needs and tasks. Human instinct is to seek creature comforts after exertion, and while Fehu can be portrayed in such a light its base concerns encompass tending to transient assets. The message here is to make sure that we have what we need.

It's a logical seasonal gearshift in that once summer arrives and all the seeds are in the ground we can turn our focus to the resources that must be managed until the crop comes in. On a soul level, perhaps *we* are the resource that must be tended. After all, the shift of season has left us new, somewhat raw, certainly revealed, and needy. It would be appropriate to consider ourselves as wealth that must be tended.

As we move from the fiery intensity of Dagaz into the shifting combustibility of Fehu, consider how we create ourselves. Under the glaring light of the season it's appropriate to examine how we use our resources to enable life as we know it and create the possibility to change it.

Fehu in its native position assures us a time of prosperity. That which we tend and nurture is in its growing season, literally and figuratively. By design this is the time of building, action, and earthly engagement.

Given the plentiful nature of the summer, it's a good time to extend self and put creative energy to work for successful outcomes. This news comes with a cautionary tale, of course. The energy of Fehu is of the Jötnar, the giants, which means it's big. Anytime the Jötnar enter the picture things are about to get wild. The Jötnar represent utangard, or wild, unknown territory. Connected to the natural forces of the Multiverse, they also represent unconscious forces within ourselves. When life force this big comes calling, it can't be ignored. It must be expressed.

Fehu is specifically indicative of assets that we must manage. Before we can manage them we must manifest them, which implies a pattern of reciprocity. We tend, harvest, reap, feed, reinvest. Such is the method of manifestation. We tend to think of manifestation in very pray-wish-poof terms, when in reality it takes quite a lot of ongoing effort. Work that must be done continually is duty. It's not just a job or task but rather what's expected of us if we wish to sustain our assets. It's what's required for the communities we participate in to continue to function well. When we don't do our individual duty we hurt the entire community.

As we realize the interwoven nature of tending our assets we're no longer merely talking about livestock, crops, or market shares. The conversation shifts to include sacred duty—that which is uniquely ours to bear and bring into being. By tending our sacred duty ongoing we remain in alignment with what's most deeply needed for the current time, our family, our community, the planet, and our souls. The result of that tending is manifesting the assets to sustain our duty.

The Sacred Self is the overseer of that duty. Called the High Self, True Self, Transpersonal Self, Big Me, use the wording that resonates with you. How you process the part of you that is in charge of your sacred duty matters. The way you name that role embodies it to do its work. Likewise if perfect balance embodies active awareness of one's Sacred Self, perfect engagement is what it takes to tend that relationship.

◆ DEVOTIONAL

Spend time daily during this half-month getting mundane affairs in order. It's incredibly difficult to cultivate a strong and sustaining spiritual practice while worried about the day-to-day. Focus on matters of practicality first. If the entire two weeks is spent managing such affairs, it's time well spent. It's always within your potential to make the mundane sacred, even if it's tallying bank balances and canning jam. Awareness follows intention.

When you're ready, take that awareness a bit further and consider your duty in the mundane. What must you do, ongoing, that left undone creates difficulty for yourself or for others? How do your assets support you to continue fulfilling that duty? Note these duties and how they affect your needs, those of your family, and those of your community.

Turn your focus inward and engage the Sacred Self. This part of you not only knows what you uniquely bring to the world, but it also has the skill set to help you tend it. For those reasons it's important to have an active alliance with this aspect of yourself. In some artistic way—song, a handwritten invitation into your life, a poem, painting—court your Sacred Self the way you would a deeply sought love. Make it an ongoing courtship, leaving daily offerings to this holy part of you. As you do so pause a few moments and find where your body feels this connection, what sensations come up. With this intended daily effort made to bring in the Sacred Self, stay open for its response.

With this aspect of you present, how do you feel? What is strange about this connection? What is comfortable?

As you feel confident walking with your Sacred Self, call in the spirit of Fehu. Ask it to step in to you and allow you to feel the cycle of tending and manifesting in your body. Where does it reside in your form? Sit with that feeling, and map it through your form, bringing awareness to any thoughts, feelings, memories, or beliefs that arise. How can you carry that feeling forward, to call on it as needed for supporting yourself?

As you become familiar with that feeling, where else do you notice it in the space around you? In your community? In the world?

To fulfill our sacred duties we must have needs met. Consider what needs must be met to fulfill your sacred duties, and state them to your Sacred Self. Do you need more self-time, money, Spirit Allies? Consider these or other needs that you need help filling.

If you have a sense of your sacred duty, journal about it. If you're unsure of it, journal about that too. As you find comfort with yourself as sacred, again note any thoughts, feelings, memories, or beliefs that come up. You don't have to judge them; just acknowledge them.

Knowing intimately the power of Fehu, what ongoing ritual is appropriate for you to do to tend your Sacred Self, to express Sacred Self in community?

In what way should you tithe, and to whom?

Fehu Half-Month Affirmation

The light shortens, slightly.
Warm brightness illuminates that
I am enough.

6
July 14–July 29
✦ Uruz ✦
Greeting Shadow

Fehu has taught us much about personal prosperity and the commitment required to sustain it. As we move into Uruz that commitment deepens. Related to the Jötnar, Audhumla—the divine feminine in the guise of the aurochs—the rune focuses our attention on associations with body, well-being, and wild potential.

It's curious that in the runic ordering we are given the opportunity to learn how to tend to our wealth before we encounter actual creation. We're given instruction on how to sustain, through Fehu, before we're fully manifest. If that isn't a significant hat tip to the importance of duty in earthly life—a.k.a. the Owner's Manual to Successful Human Life—I don't know what is. As Uruz is associated with Audhumla, it's a significant force of creation. Because there's no indication of how she originated she's seen as having created herself. She's seen as eternal, thus sustaining in her support of us. With Uruz we are such infinite mysteries as well.

Our short time with her brings an important observation of vitality. In this season we have the opportunity to make use of our faculties to our highest capability and have the support of an omnipotent force while we do so. This is a natural time to expect and find physical support. It's a time that the body's ability to self-heal is exalted, and any changes we implement toward that goal will be fortified by the elements.

With the associations of Audhumla creating herself into form, Uruz is very much steeped in all things body and sexuality. With form being our most obvious state of self, we take for granted that we know our bodies, and New Age pop culture still passively teaches us to deny our physicality in favor of our souls. Such a philosophy isn't at all different from concepts of original sin or the denial of base human needs. For that reason the part of ourselves that we least often know isn't the soul but our body and its most powerful consciousness counterpart— our ego. If body is the altar of who we are, ego is its guardian. When we sit in ignorance of the ego we sit in ignorance of Shadow, which is our greatest mystery.

Where Fehu represents domesticated cattle, Uruz is the wild, untamable aurochs, and as such, brings us close to parts of ourselves that we've been taught to subdue, if not subvert. More dominant and demanding than feelings, unconscious motivators are usually internalized before we're even verbal. They express themselves as Freudian slips, acting without clear motivation, acting without realizing the action, irrational fear, and so on. Uruz brings our attention to these seemingly minor behaviors as places to generate radical change. When we become consciously aware of them, and thus take back control of them, we integrate them into informed choice. We stand with more information and can focus the energy and change we want to make in our lives and the world. We do that by engaging Shadow.

Shadow is our greatest intrigue, not because it is unknowable but because we most often desire not to know it. We evade working with it because it seems frightening, or it may reveal aspects of ourselves too dark for us to handle. In reality Shadow is merely what isn't lit. It's what we don't know about ourselves. Once revealed it's no longer Shadow.

Uruz harnesses the ability to sit in the space between knowing impeccably who we are and having no idea. It fosters our ability to dwell in our thought-space and create ourselves as we want to be, which is born of learning who we've been. This stave is wild potential, magick at its rawest.

Bear in mind that Uruz is the creative force, not what is created.

◆ DEVOTIONAL

For this devotional find a quiet, dark indoor space that supports a still mind. Gather fetishes, items of meaning and power, to place about the space as you relax. Turn off the phone, the television. If appropriate, cover your eyes with a scarf to blot distraction.

Close your eyes and imagine comfort in the darkness that greets you. In the furthest reaches of your imagination, wrap snug in that darkness. Allow nothing else, for now.

In this safe, hallowed space invite in the aspect of you most needing your attention. Still focused only on the darkness, honor this part of you. Welcome it as you would a long-lost loved one. Bless it as you would someone who has given you the best news ever. Forgive it passionately as you would someone who'd harmed you yet you desperately love. Ask it to forgive you as you would someone you'd hurt terribly, who needs you to see your integrity. Express love to this part of you, heartfelt and pure. Finally, receive it as you would the best gift on your favorite holiday.

Let this aspect of you ease into your senses. Observe how it feels, how it appears. Remain open to what it needs to convey to you and allow the depth of exchange necessary to listen and be heard. If healing is needed for either of you, call Audhumla in to facilitate that rite. Honor her presence, and ask her for the healing that's needed. When it's done, ask how to maintain that healing. Be sure to thank her and ask what offerings you can make on her behalf.

> ### Uruz Half-Month Affirmation
>
> I am my Shadow.
> In knowing all of me,
> I am free to be.

7
July 29–August 13
◆ Thurisaz and Lammas ◆
Finding Personal Divinity

Lammas / Lughnasadh, the first-harvest sabbat, comes as we emerge from deep within ourselves. Most celebrate it around August 1, though the calculated date falls when the sun reaches 15 degrees of Leo. Generally speaking, the acknowledgment of reaping early spoils of spring planting is appropriate throughout this half-month.

As Uruz drew us deeper into matters of the unconscious, Thurisaz puts us on alert to stand in what we learned there. The power of the natural laws and their ability to radically change our lives is never more present than through Thurisaz. The third rune of the first ætt, it comes from the Old Norse word *thursar,* meaning "devourer." Chaotic forces that can consume us are at hand.

As it is associated with Thor, and "thorn," this stave is prickly. While we'd like to think its barbs caught us out of nowhere, most likely they are the result of some unrequited need that lurked at the edge of our consciousness until it exploded. While it may flare like Mjölnir's lightning strike, ultimately we can't pretend that we didn't see it coming.

Therein lie the protective aspects of this rune as well. Things are usually unconscious for a reason: we couldn't process them at their inception, we didn't have the developmental faculties to create a formidable narrative around them, and so forth. They're big, in short.

They're so big that we have to shelve them a bit before we can be certain of healthily managing them into our waking awareness. The truth of Thurisaz is that the shadows are coming. It may as well be on our terms.

Anything that has the potential to consume us can destroy us. If the Jötnar are primal forces that can devour us, then Thurisaz is our heads-up to be proactive about that outcome. The progression of the first staves of the first ætt shows awareness that we must always tend to ourselves (Fehu). We can't be stale in how we manifest, no matter what's going on around us. Uruz enforced that we have innate power to control the process of how we create ourselves—no matter what's going on within us. Thurisaz, then, brings in the double-edged awareness that there are other forces in play that can radically alter our personal plan for manifestation yet still stay behind the wheel in how it all plays out. We can't let go of the wheel, no matter the actions or choices of others around us. This is the devourer/thorn/self-directed change nature of Thurisaz. While some see the strike of Thor's hammer as the unexpected force that knocks down the dominoes, I see it as the reminder amid the fallout that we can still have a say in how we recover.

Maybe it's both.

The preparation for the initiation at hand has been to embrace the Sacred Self (Fehu) and Shadow (Uruz). Through the Sacred Self devotion we've glimpsed our own vast depths then honored Shadow. The most terrifying aspects of Shadow aren't unsavory parts of ourselves we can't stomach; rather they're the most powerful, most empowered aspects of ourselves that we most fear. Culturally we assume that if we glimpse ourselves as powerful then we can no longer also have faults. We can't conceive of ourselves as a work in progress and hold the nuances of wisdom, experience, and value.

This stave doesn't spell disaster and ruin. It portends the need to hold dynamics gently and have the willingness to redirect them as needed. Think organically and act or react openly. There is no room for habit. The core of Thurisaz is the reminder not to become rote, not to be stuck in "getting by." It's not easy for every aspect of our lives to be inspired or to make the calls that distinguish what we are heart-drawn to do from what we must accomplish. However that's exactly what we must do now. To do that, to see that distinction, we must change how we see ourselves. It is the most bountiful harvest we can behold.

◆ LAMMAS INITIATION

Lammas begins the first of eight runic sabbat initiations. In a private, quiet space gather a few fetishes, powerful items symbolizing your personal power. They may be trinkets, colors, textures, scents, music, stones—things that when you experience them you feel yourself in your power. Arrange them with yourself in a circle, such that you face them as part of the circle.

Also include a physical representation of something you've created, something you are most proud to have brought to the world. It may be the yield of your garden, a photo of your family, artwork you've produced, or a symbol of hard-won healing within. Place it in the center of the circle.

If necessary to shift in to a more altered state, engage in fire breathing for a count of fifty. Breathing only through the mouth, close your eyes and inhale more deeply than usual, and exhale more deeply than usual, very quickly. Blow the breaths out forcefully, as if you are blowing them away from you. This style of breathing allows you to drop in to light trance quickly.

Take a few moments to connect with the items that help you to feel your power. Speak aloud the reason you've included each, what feelings it stirs, and what component of power each represents for you. Maybe some bring mental clarity, joy, passion, or fun. Let yourself be filled with whatever qualities they bring that translate into power.

When you're ready, move your focus to the item in the center of the circle, the symbol of what your power has created. Speak aloud and in detail what this item is, what it represents, and how it has allowed you to express your power. When you are ready, ask the spirit of this item to come into the circle.

Observe its characteristics—colors, composure, feel. Express gratitude for its place in your life and for all the things that helped you to bring it into being. Ask this spirit what it needs you to know in return. Ask what it needs.

When you feel ready, ask the personal power that resides within you to enter the circle. Observe how your body feels as you behold this powerful part of you. Sense what qualities define this part of you, what values. Note how it feels similar or different from the life forces already present in the circle.

Take a few moments to sing to the aspects of power holding space with you. Allow yourself to be wrapped in the feeling of your power beholding you as you do it. Allow yourself to realize these parts of your power that you carry at all times, consciously and unconsciously. As you sense them, remind yourself that they are always accessible. They are always part of you.

At this time thank all the aspects of you who have shown up as your power, who continue to show up. Thank your conscious and unconscious minds for their willingness to work together for your success. Thank yourself for your willingness to find harvest within yourself.

The most difficult harvest to honor is that born of our own labor. Lammas is the time of internalizing the delicate rhythm of realizing that, for all our efforts, natural forces beyond our control are at work. Whether it's literally the garden and weather, or self-work and life, we only have so much control over how it will all come out. We plant the seeds, tend them the best we can, and hope for the best. Yet our true stance of power isn't in hovering over the process and judging the outcome. It's in putting in the elbow grease, realizing our adaptability, getting out of the way of the process, and allowing what manifests. The ability to truly carry that stance through life requires that we see our true selves—our own divinity—reflected in that process. We see that we are as involved as we are not. We see that the outcome is as determined by us as it is by other influences.

This is all you need to know about your role in creation, power, and manifestation.

This is all you will ever need to know about them.

Take careful notes on what you brought to the circle, your reasons for doing so, and the spirit of power that united each of them. If this is your first initiation with Thurisaz record thoughts of who you have been across life, who you have learned that you are in the past month. If you're repeating the Thurisaz Lammas initiation note how you see yourself has changed since the first encounter.

As you journal, consider the following:

Having delved into deeper aspects of yourself over the past month, how do you view your creative process now? Over what parts of it do you have control? In what ways can you lessen a need for control?

Examine any crises Thurisaz brought up. How do they relate to your feelings about personal power?

In what way do your creations reflect you? Do you reflect them?

How will you approach the first harvest next year? How would you use the devotional time differently? The same?

> ### *Thurisaz Half-Month Affirmation*
>
> In my creations
> I behold myself
> As you.

8
August 13–August 29
✦ Ansuz ✦
Speaking Your Personal Truth

The time after the first harvest is a quieter one. There is a downhill feeling of lots having been cast as well as reaping what may come of them. In this gentler moment we come into the refined breeze of Ansuz—refreshment in time for the dog days of August.

Often called Odin's rune, Ansuz is the fourth rune in the first ætt. In the native order of the Elder Futhark it's the first point that we move away from giant energy and step in to something more ethereal. In these waning days of summer we greet Asgard.

Having moved through the base laws of Nature we arrive at the point that divinity happens—hence the stave's association with Odin. Often regarded as meaning "mouth," it more aptly indicates "breath," as the divine force that moves through All Things. In fact it doesn't just move through—as in animate—it gives us the power to draw on that force and create with it. We gain the mental process of figuring out what we want to say, and we have the mechanisms in place to do just that. In short, Ansuz represents a simple force and the complicated process required to make masterful use of it. In this way Ansuz is associated with the breath of Odin.

What Odin, seen as the god of gods, said came to be. As in many cultural creation stories, in the Old Norse tradition Odin's spell-song brought what we know as reality into being. Thoughtforms are the precursors to reality. Word is power, and coming into the knowledge that we embody that same power makes it incredibly provocative.

Having found our divinity through the Lammas initiation we must face the reality that what we say *is* as well. Through the sticky, shadow motivations of the giants, Ansuz is the voice of reason, or the ability to apply logic to those inner processes and desires. It's a way for us to focus our intent. Of course Ansuz doesn't automatically bring clarity of intent or an innate understanding of what we really want. There's work to be done there.

Ansuz is the point that we begin to ascribe words to all the crazy, wonderful, wild things inside us. Again, we have to know what words we want to use to describe ourselves and our desires, feelings, intentions. If we don't know—if we're just blank—it goes nowhere. If we don't know or are confused and use the wrong words we get garbled unintended results. When we start to look we see what Ansuz is really asking us to do—it's to be careful what we name things. It's to allow that internal percolation, the culling of this or that, here or there, hell yes or hell no. Because when we are active in that primal simmering self-engagement—not just being brutalized by anxiety over it—we come away with real, tangible kernels of truth about who we are, what we want, how to bring that to the world, and how to engender support to continue doing that. Through this stave we take ownership of the entire creative process. Ideally having done that healing and releasing early in the process, we become not only more aware of what's actually within our capability but also what work is required on our part to sustain the song.

Thus Ansuz emphasizes speaking our truth, which can be seen as a form of soothsaying. When we combine the delicate lightness of words with the potency of our power, they become spells. They become prophecy. With the season of Ansuz arrives the point that we can't just live as this divine being on the inside. We can't sustain merely an internalized ecstatic, escapist trip. In fact Ansuz informs us that we were never meant to do that; rather we must bring our divinity to the world. We must express it, and we must do so *well*.

Such is the message of this season. This rune carries the powers of a spell. Knowing how, when, and where to evoke just the right words for what we want is key to its magick, as is realizing the impact of what we say on the world around us. Since it follows the early harvest, Ansuz sets our expectations for what comes as the weather cools. For this half-month be careful what's wished for. This is the native time of words' empowerment.

◆ DEVOTIONAL

As you journal for this half-month jot down words that best describe you and detail your logic for applying them to yourself.

Afterward make a list of personal truths. They can be anything, from describing a calling to talents, convictions, preferences.

Finally, make a list of what inspires you. Be as detailed as necessary to fully describe and feel the inspiration of these words while you write them.

As you write these words notice what sensations and feelings they stir in your body and note those as well. For instance, "When I honor that I'm a kickass martial artist, I feel heat in my chest and my body feels more strong."

How does the feeling of inspiration differ from the feeling of your personal power (as with Thurisaz)? How is it the same?

By stating truths and sensing where they stir us we somatically learn what it feels like to be aligned with the magick of creativity. As we connect words with feelings we map that neurological reaction through our bodies. When we feel it, we carry it with us and can re-create it at any time, in any place. The ability to carry that mapping everywhere we go enables us to detect untruths when we encounter them, because they take us out of that word-feeling map. We then know, by association, that disconnection equals untruth. We also know that when we want to create something for ourselves we can call on that feeling and ask its name.

Take some time during this half-month to consider that the feelings elicited when inspired and the feelings of personal empowerment come from the same source. Pair them with feelings and sensations to create powerful outcomes.

Ansuz Half-Month Affirmation

The more clearly I think and feel,
The more impeccably I speak,
The more capable I am.

9
August 29–September 13
◆ Raidho ◆
Telling Your Story

Summer is officially winding down, and Raidho prepares the way for the second-harvest sabbat, Mabon. In anticipation of that initiation we encounter the need to be very clear in how we tell our stories.

Raidho is translated as "travel," as in the act of movement, of getting from Point A to Point B. We're often told it's the journey that matters, not the destination; however I think Raidho is proof positive that both are equally important. Metaphorically this stave speaks of seeing the best move and taking it, which is in essence being in flow with All Things. Raidho embodies the application of the wisdom earned from preceding runes, which creates directed motion. With the culmination at Raidho we realize our capability of focused life force in balance with the life force of All Things.

This rune suggests the ability to take all of that personal insight and experience and project them alongside the rhythm of the Multiverse. What's significant about this meshing of influences is that every path is unique. No two of our paths will or can be the same; thus our relationship to All Things isn't the same. Each of our journeys is different. There's profound power in realizing just how much choice we have in life, the freedom we have to express it and still remain in sync with the world dance. In essence we can't screw it up, and Raidho encourages us to drop the judgment that we can. There's no such thing as off the path.

Yes, we can make pit stops, take turns that weren't originally intended, lag behind some predetermined expectation, get blindsided, or totally change direction. Any and all of the aforementioned can occur, and we're still on course. In this way Raidho typifies the notion that we can't veer off our spiritual path. Get distracted, maybe. Become confused from time to time. But never totally go off course. We take what comes in stride, though not necessarily elegantly, and we keep moving down the road.

When viewed this way Raidho is about how we tell our story. It's the trip we took, the experience we had, and how we share that story with the world. It's how we manifest our ideals and create lore for how we move forward in them.

The nuance to that progression is finding comfort in the tension between our experience and what of it we share, between what is our fate and what is our choice. Where the storytelling aspect of Raidho becomes its own force is in deciding which is which. Even when we know which is which, what of the two are actually attainable? What is the way we must go versus the way we want to go? Which is the path our heart sings and the one that's actually available to us? What is profession versus calling? What choices do we have, as opposed to what ones we should create? This is the real meaty stuff of storytelling, and for most of us it is a tension that we carry throughout life. So even though Raidho has a very feel-good vibe and no-harm precedent where one's life path is concerned, its season places heavy emphasis on our ability to master it.

In that light it's not the story of ourselves that we're telling but how we're reacting to the story we're living. Are they the same? Should they be?

◆ DEVOTIONAL

Create a timeline of the traveling you have done through your life, in as much detail as is needed, birth to present. Note significant trips you took or even short excursions. Where did you go? What did you do there? What was most memorable? Who traveled with you, and who did you meet at your destinations? What left you breathless and inspired? If shadows and sadness arose, what stirred them?

When you've gotten them down, go back through each trip and note the condition of your life after you came home. What was different? What was the same? Who were you?

Who are you now?

Raidho Half-Month Affirmation

The story I tell,
The story I live,
Create the story I am.

10
September 13–September 28
✦ Kenaz and Mabon ✦
Meeting the Personal Metaphor

As Kenaz brings culmination to the manifestation process in the first ætt, so Mabon is the second-harvest sabbat, which emphasizes that we reap what we sow. Just as the summer season has given us bounty that helps us determine direction for the coming cold season, the runes of the first ætt have set us up for similar insight. The Autumnal Equinox occurs when the sun moves directly over the equator, making the duration of light and darkness almost equal. For most, this point occurs sometime between September 22 and 24.

If we think of the progression of Ansuz, Raidho, and Kenaz as a formula for focusing our creative vision, it would look something like this:

Soothsaying + Storytelling = Meaning
Ansuz + Raidho = Kenaz

Where Ansuz has brought the ability to harness internal processes to know what we think then articulate it, Raidho has given us the ability to formulate those concepts into a narrative that shapes how we see ourselves and the self that we present to the world. With Kenaz we begin to understand why.

With all this discussion of words and expression it should come as no surprise that Kenaz is the rune of kenning. Kenning is a poetic way of speaking that involves referring metaphorically to something, thereby evoking a deeper response than merely referring to the thing itself. Where it's easy to just say the word we mean, kenning evokes a more dramatic effect, literally using more words than necessary. In this way this meaning of Kenaz also imparts a sense of buildup, of extra, of tipping over. I'll go so far as to say that kenning induces a theta brain state, or shamanic ecstasy. It allows us to pair deeply moving language with feeling and action so that one's calling becomes a "heart song." Kenaz itself is "shadow lighter." Through kenning we offer a description of the thing, which allows us to relate to it. It evokes our feelings about the thing.

In addition, Kenaz is related to keening, or wails that indicate pain. Some translations of this stave connect it with a small, niggling fire, and it's this tie with keening that gives it the undertones of a boil simmering beneath the skin. In this way Kenaz presents a necessity of having to deal with a situation that left unattended gets worse.

In this progression of creative voyage there's no emphasis on where we actually went, what we actually did, how we did it, who accompanied us, what went well, what blew up in our faces. Those are the details that we as humans tend to dwell on, but the runes couldn't care less about those minutiae; rather they emphasize finding what we *learned* from the experience.

Kenaz is that which must be expressed. It's burning passion that comes from our deepest fusion of creativity and practical knowledge, none of which will abate until it's released upon the world. Given that, Kenaz indicates self-derived inspiration, the aha moment born of long-sought clarity.

Kenaz is the synthesis of the unconscious and the conscious. Years ago a friend introduced me to the idea of micro-thoughts—slight insights that provoke thinking from just at the edge of awareness, and then at the point of provocation, vanish. Most often the crux of them is forgotten, though the passion of them lingers, continuing to trump more dominant thoughts until they flash into full revelation. This season brings a natural time to bring some pushed-back need or idea to the fore. The elements are in place to do so safely and vividly. Kenaz isn't concerned with how neatly we allow the revelation or whether we have the skills to execute it. It just wants us to face something we've known for a long time, and kinda sorta tortured ourselves over.

◆ MABON SABBAT INITIATION

Old Norse culture has the concept of the *hamr,* or a second self that takes on another form. It's part of our earthly self, though its key ability is to travel the astral plane in search of wisdom, healing, or aid that's needed. In this way the hamr has its own life, with strengths, abilities, knowledge, wisdom. It travels voluntarily. However, without recognizing the hamr and intentionally forming direct relationship with it, we can't engage it in a way of benefit to us or to it. When we seek intentional relationship with it, we can enlist it to help us find specific help that we need in life.

Take some time to write out exactly what your strengths and skills are. Be explicit. Likewise note life areas in which you excel. When you've detailed these, note areas in which you don't feel as skilled and knowledge-able, or life areas in which you'd like help or insight.

In a quiet space verify that this work is right for you to pursue at this time. If it isn't, consult the part(s) of you that voices concern, and do the work needed to address that concern.

Much as you invited Shadow with Uruz, take a moment to find comfort in realizing another part of yourself that may be less familiar. If any tension arises at the thought, allow it to be. Inhale, placing your focus as far back into your memory of when the tension began as possible. From that source, exhale through its feeling in the present, and repeat that pattern of breathing until the body relaxes, until feelings about the idea of bringing forward another part of you are arise. If it takes a few attempts to accomplish finding a peaceful state, allow the time. There's no rush.

As you feel comfort in your body, in the space you've created, sense where you start and stop. Begin at your heart, and allow your awareness to drift slowly lower and wider, to your knees, above your head, beyond your fingertips, under your feet. Gradually feel the boundary of yourself, then increase your awareness to expand outward and wrap around you. As your awareness expands beyond your body, allow your focus to explore that boundary. If awareness veers out so much that you begin to lose focus, draw the boundary nearer. Ask it to come just beyond your fingers and toes.

When you find the barrier between yourself and the space hosting you, observe what that boundary feels like. What separates you from the space around you? What similarities or differences do you notice between yourself and the space?

When you feel comfortable in that knowledge, speak aloud thus, "I walk with All That I am. I protect and care for All That I am, always." Use wording that is most natural to you, making sure to convey to your physical, mental, and emotional layers the intention that whatever aspects of self you explore, you do so with the good of it all in mind. However, mean what you say. When we venture into etheric strata, it's easy to want to chase after what we find there—even helpful aspects of self—with disregard for what's central to our total well-being. Whatever wording you use, convey it with the intention of full protection, care, and compassion for self.

With this vow in place, ask your hamr to step in to the space you've created. As you begin to sense it, note its characteristics. How does it present itself to you? Go with whatever comes, through all of your senses. How do you feel as you behold it? Take a few moments to observe it and check your feelings against those observations. What part of this being is familiar? What part is strange?

Introduce yourself to your hamr. Recall your strengths and skills and present them to this being as gifts for it to use, as needed. Present your physical state of being as such as well. Likewise reveal to it the places in which you need support.

Let your hamr express itself through your form, as it needs. With your focus still on what is safe and within your capability to bear, give the hamr sound, movement, and access to your senses. What sense do you have of its capabilities? What spaces does it have access to that you do not?

It may take several sittings with your hamr to generate a dialogue. As you become able to foster that interaction, tend it, ongoing. Create this relationship as one of reciprocity. For everything you ask of your hamr, offer something in return.

This is the part of you that is beyond you. It carries skills and wisdom you need, just as you embody expression and engagement not native to your hamr. For now leave your hamr with an agreement to engage it at some regular interval—weekly, twice a week. Create space in your life for this relationship, and stay observant of how your mundane life gets shaped around it.

Ultimately in sharing form with your hamr it is your life that is shape-shifted.

As you process this work consider what wisdom of the past couple of months is burning to be carried forward? What insight smolders to burst into full light? This is your Mabon harvest.

I often tell my shamanic students, "Shamanism is where you stand. It isn't another place, culture, or time. You're already on the path. Learn to be in direct relationship with it. Learn who is standing there."

Indeed, who stands on your path?

Kenaz Half-Month Affirmation

As I expand knowing who I am,
I come to know
Comfort in my unknowable.

11
September 28–October 13
✦ Gebo ✦
Giving and Growing

When Gebo appears in personal readings for clients I tell them that this is one of the staves everyone wants in their cast. It brings a general light tone, sense of partnership and balance, and it promotes exchange and elements of closure. This stave is such a lovely truth. It speaks to all things related to partnership, gifts, and balanced exchange. Sayings often associated with Gebo are "A gift for a gift" and "A gift freely given." In modern minds, they seem to conflict. How can a gift be freely given if there's always the underlying expectation of receiving one as well? How can we receive a gift with no angst if we are expected to reciprocate?

The Old Norse *Hávamál* expresses a great deal about our relationship to everything in life, not just to each other, and summarizes Gebo perfectly:

> *Better ask for too little than offer too much,*
> *like the gift should be the boon;*
> *better not to send than to overspend.*[1]

In the *Hávamál,* Odin discusses the significance of even exchange, not just with the literal gift given but the process of giving it as well. It's just as important not to expect to get anything back as it is to give, express gratitude, and not overextend oneself to start with. It's not just about getting and giving, but the ritual itself.

If we're not poised to give in good faith, don't.

If it will deplete us to give, don't.

In this way there's a lot more going on with Gebo than is initially revealed. This self-preservation current is part of its inherent emphasis on balance. As with exchanges with other people this teaching espouses wisdom regarding coming into relationship with enlightenment. We must understand what we're getting in to when we begin on a path of awakening. When we undertake such a study—as the runes—it can't be done by halves. We give ourselves over to it, or we are done in by it. This is the balance component of Gebo that is often overlooked.

Indeed Gebo heralds the perfect time to enjoy the waning harvest season. The current of this stave is learning to do for self as it benefits the collective—meaning that our actions must bless beyond merely ourselves. It's okay to focus on personal needs and to honor them; however we must do so in a way that benefits others with the same need. I find this approach to self-care and community responsibility incredibly powerful and empowering, particularly now, when the planet demands it.

Gebo, as does this harvest season, asks us to go deep into our sense of what we can give, what we should give, what we must accept, and how to sustain balance through it all. Despite how supportive that all sounds, balance is particularly difficult to achieve in challenging times. The ultimate memo for this half-month is that we are supported. Our task is to figure out what we can give to get through challenges and become educated in what we lack.

◆ DEVOTIONAL

Change is how we grow, and many—if not all—of the runes challenge our comfort with the degrees of change we're willing to make and in what areas of life. Gebo is one such spot that we can experience the change generated from balanced exchange and partnership.

As you galdr Gebo and consider the gifts you receive, and those you give, explore your feelings about sacrifice. What does it mean to you? What are you willing to sacrifice in order to grow? What are you willing to accept in order to grow?

> ### *Gebo Half-Month Affirmation*
>
> How I give,
> What I accept,
> Feeds my community.

12
October 13–October 28
◆ Wunjo ◆
Allowing Joy

Transitioning from Gebo to Wunjo brings a relatively peaceful time. These staves wind down the first ætt, which means a brief reprieve. The completion of the first ætt on the seasonal wheel brings a time of realization of the hard work that's been put in, newfound respect for how challenging it is to be a spirit in form, and finding the joy in that challenging process. It is a *process,* however, which means the blissful lull won't last long.

With Gebo I noted that it's one of the staves everyone wants in their casts. Wunjo is the other. Indeed it comes after a period of hard work, and its traditionally accepted meaning is "joy." It's a state of being in tune with one's wyrd and all the many factors that influence who we are and the choices we make. More than being aware of our place in the process, it's realizing our power in the process—how much we have and how little we have—and being okay with both. In fact it's being so okay with both that we're thankful for that vantage point.

There's this idea that Wunjo is offered up for free, or is there to be taken. The thing about joy is that it's not a given. Some people have the perspective that it's abundantly floating around in the Multiverse, or that it's a reward. The placement of Wunjo in the traditional ordering of the Elder Futhark points to joy being realized. Sure it's out there at any given time, but we must be in the state of being, head, and heart to see it for what it is, allow ourselves to experience it, and stand solid in that moment. Looking at it that way, joy is a far more personal and subjective thing.

Joy is out there. It's possible to brush against it, breathe it, wallow in it. Now's the reminder that regardless of what has come and what lies ahead, one should give oneself the opportunity to find joy in it. However small or fleeting, we all deserve as much joy as we can give ourselves.

Wunjo is peaceful, however given its place at the end of the first ætt, this closure stave hints that having learned how to energetically fend for ourselves in form, we'll take reprieve when it's presented. But will we? That's the thing about joy. It's ever there, though whether we choose to allow it draws on an entirely other set of skills. The message as we move closer to the final-harvest sabbat, closer to the Dark Time, is that when we have the opportunity for joy and don't take it, or refuse to take it, that choice may spin out repercussions all its own.

♦ DEVOTIONAL

What represented joy to you when you were five years old? Over the next two weeks pay close attention to your laughter, your allowance for frivolity. Set aside at least one occasion to celebrate the way you experienced joy as a child. Allow this time to do something you enjoyed as a child though have missed as an adult, maybe something that specifically isn't "allowed" for adults. Invite others who can share the fun if it feels right to do so.

How do you allow yourself joy? What emotions do you associate with joy? Where do you sense it in your body? As you galdr Wunjo, what comes up?

When you can map joy through your feelings and body you internalize it in such a way that you can recall those feelings and re-create its sensations any time you need them. The state of joy is a mindfulness practice as much as any other. The more you engage it, the more easily joy is recognized and felt.

> ### Wunjo Half-Month Affirmation
> I can give others,
> And I can allow myself,
> The option of joy.

13
October 28–November 13
✦ Hagalaz and Samhain ✦
Facing Fear, Finding Faith

Samhain is widely observed on October 31 in the north, though its cal-culated date is based on the sun reaching 15 degrees of Scorpio, which is in early November. In the Southern Hemisphere it is widely celebrated on May 1, which lies on the opposite side of the runic wheel. Samhain is the Celtic name given to the first day of winter. It corresponds with the Old Norse Winter Nights, or *vetrnætr,* which is a several-night transi-tion between fall and winter.

Closing the harvest sabbats is Samhain. It's the time of discerning which animals will be kept and which slaughtered. What of the crops' yield can be gleaned has been stored for the rough winter ahead and reserved for planting in the coming year.

Spiritually speaking dark influences weren't considered evil in Old Norse culture. This time of year brought Alfablót, or sacrifice to the elves, which usually took the form of portions of beer or meat. In the Northern Tradition honoring the elves was an opportunity to get on the good side of Nature Spirits and Ancestors who would help communities with-stand the harsh winter. A time of endings, it's also a time of uncertainty, in that darkness presses in, and the cold of limited light is heralded by Hagalaz. The first of the winter trio of runes—Hagalaz, Nauthiz, and Isa—this stave translates as "hail," a frozen state between states. Quite literally, as this rune is associated with the god Heimdallr, a sentinel of order stationed at the cusp where the worlds of deities and humans meet, thoughts of a grander plan are attributed to this time of year. As Samhain is considered a time between times it seems appropriate that the stave enlivened during this season would be about the between.

Bear in mind as well that we shift from the formative, manifestation currents of the first ætt, which ended with the blissful high note of Wunjo, to this harsh welcome into the second ætt. This jagged transition hints at impermanence. Life is change, and as we can't cling to joy we must be able to hold it loosely even as we venture beyond it into what comes next. Such transitions are why we cultivate mindfulness. They are why we map our feelings into our bodies so that we can exercise habits to support us through change. Hagalaz, and the winter runes in general, are all about change.

The modern pagan history lesson on Samhain is always about fear and uncertainty. We don't face the challenges of Nature that our ancestors did, so we don't readily appreciate those states of being and how they relate to the season. We have relatively climate-controlled lives, neutralizing the influence of the elements on our instincts and to some degree our resources. Our ancestors faced genuine distress in the long cold, including concerns about starvation and cabin fever. Because we're detached from such concerns it can be easy to forget that such extremes were part of life for them. Despite the fact that we don't live under those conditions, we have manifested the distress response to the colder season in seasonal affective disorder (SAD). It is appropriate this time of year that we consider our personal reactions to the season and implement supports for self-caregiving.

Faith is important in times of darkness. It is a belief, a hope, and a pledge to something greater than what is known. In that light faith holds utmost regard for the unknown, which is the focus of Samhain.

We know that Heimdallr's function at Bifröst is to separate the world of gods and goddesses from the human world, but for what reason? Part of the human plight is coming to terms with what we don't know, which we accomplish through scientific research, spiritual exploration, venturing into interrelationship with other beings. Ours is a quest to know, yet the barrier of Heimdallr continually reiterates the message of what we can't know. Through his firm stance at the door between we realize not just the unknown but the unknowable as well.

Despite that cool impossibility, human consciousness is continuously drawn to the warmth of possible enlightenment. There persists the idea that Beyond is better, that souls out of form hold greater wisdom, and that such insight is attainable through application of the right measures. Depending on personal boundaries the process of gaining that insight can be noble, or disturbing. Ultimately ours is a life spiritually empowered, though we have to choose to see it that way. We have to realize we are gods as well.

Most often though we get stuck on the hamster wheel of thinking that deities are better and thus hold a status we can never achieve. The ancient Norse powers that be recognized this conundrum and installed Heimdallr on the Bifröst—the Rainbow Bridge separating the world of humans from the world of gods—with good reason. The role of gods and goddesses is to keep the worlds of their charges balanced. To maintain that balance they must remain objective and emotionally detached from the worlds they guard. The role of humanity is to explore formed Nature. That exploration can only take place with emotion, passion, excitement, fury—everything but detachment. To perform these diverse roles the paths of humans and gods cannot intersect. If deities gained emotion and became entrenched in the affairs of form, balance would be disrupted. If humans became privy to the machinations of the gods, the ensuing mental and emotional crises would impair the exploration of form. Beyond their rightful bounds each half of the polarity ceases to sustain its function. With neither holding its proper space the role of each in wyrd—how we engage the laws of Nature—is obscured. Chaos ensues.

With that internalized human purpose at the fore, falling back in love with the rickety reality that is life in form is the focus of Samhain, and it is a feat that requires deep faith. We must have faith that the sun will return, that we will grow and thrive beyond our present understanding at a pace that is healthy for us. For that rightful initiation to occur we must face our fears about the dark times in our lives. In facing those fears, we find their light.

As this is a time of death, hibernation, and order, so it is right to create our own structure for observing the teachings of this sabbat.

Also worth noting is that none of the winter runes can be reversed. Their wisdom cannot be bypassed, their experiences can't be avoided.

◆ SAMHAIN SABBAT INITIATION

Prepare to create in form your fear of lack and uncertainty. For this initiation choose an avenue of artistic expression that challenges you. For instance, painters should choose a medium other than painting. Writers should choose a medium other than writing. The purpose of this recapitulation is to move through the synapses in a new way to access these fears and bring them into form. When we attempt to do such work through known synaptic pathways we hide from ourselves. We edit. By working with these feelings in a less-honed approach, we tap in to raw consciousness and create wild expression.

A few days in advance gather the instruments needed to create this art. Likewise plan a safe place to light a fire with the capacity to transmute this artistic creation. Gather the supplies needed to start and tend the fire with care. Plan to have water nearby.

Begin this work at Samhain's sunset, as it is determined for your location. Carried on the shadowed wings of the Dark Time and with the fortitude of Hagalaz's ability to break away from the old and find new order, you will be able to give form to the story of your fears and uncertainties by creating them in art.

Throughout the process of creating this piece of art, hold in mind the fears and uncertainties to be released. Every stroke, every line cast into this art not only doubts about what can come but also doubts about what is. Let go of the story of self that has been told, that no longer holds truth. Allow whatever thoughts, feelings, or memories that get stirred to become part of this artwork. However fear is demonstrated, incorporate its symbols into your artwork—colors, animals, scenes.

Allow it to take as long as it takes.

When completed escort the artwork to the location of your fire. Start the fire, and when it is stoked to a sustainable flame, welcome it into your space.

Behold the creation and honor the depths that rendered it. Engage fire breathing for a count of fifty. Breathing only through the mouth, close your eyes and inhale more deeply than usual, and exhale more deeply than usual, very quickly. Blow the breaths out forcefully, as if you are blowing them away from you.

As you edge closer to trance, call in the heart of yourself, however you define that.

Call in the heart of the fire, and let it present itself to you as it requires.

Call in the spirit of the artwork you have created.

Express to the artwork's spirit your intention of releasing it back to Nature, through flame. Thank it for what it has brought to your life. Ask it what healing it needs from you, as part of this release. Call in your Spirit Allies to fill this need, and give healing. You don't have to engage the healing; witnessing is enough. As you feel led, sing the galdr of Hagalaz, feeling gratitude for order, for life betwixt, and for the transmutation of one thing into another.

When your allies complete healing the spirit of the artwork, ask them to heal you.

When this healing is complete, offer the art to the fire. Release the art and its legacy to Nature. Like no other element, fire typifies destruction and clears the path for new growth. Sit with the burning of what is no longer needed and be warmed in its glow. Let the illuminating light fill the spaces left from what was removed. Imagine it flowing through your body, around it, above the crown, and beneath the feet.

With that sense of enlightened fullness express gratitude for fire, for the ability to find warmth when it's needed, and for the wisdom to create release when it's time. Honor yourself for allowing this new chapter in your personal story and for engaging a fresh channel in wyrd.

Allow the sensations of openness. There's no requirement to retrieve the past, find new beliefs, or hold any particular thoughts or feelings. All that is needed is to be fully present in this moment.

When you and the fire find compatible warmth, come back to your breathing, and open your eyes. As you move on from this initiation in the days to come take the ashes from the fire and offer them to the earth. Bury them in a cherished flowerbed or garden spot. Keep nothing of this creation other than the freedom it has given you. Offer the ashes as support to feed new life elsewhere.

In journaling about the Dark Time and Hagalaz, of breathing this between space, consider the following:

How do you find your center and sway with it?
How do you create from faith to build the future?

Hagalaz Half-Month Affirmation

Between darkness and light
Is the wisdom of balance,
The embrace of peaceful unknown.

14
November 13–November 28
✦ Nauthiz ✦
Embracing Need

Hagalaz began the Dead Time, in which we are now firmly entrenched. The energy has shifted from any tingly thinning of the veil to full-on life in the shadows. The tugs we feel personally and collectively to either crawl under the covers and stay there or charge the king's gate are real. Dealing in needs and rebellious streaks, Nauthiz is a study in the extremes over which we are most often agonizing, smack in the middle.

As do all the winter runes, Nauthiz calls our attention to betwixt states. As it is the middle rune of the chilly trio, it represents a bound position and the tension that comes with it. Indeed it's the latter with which we most identify. Often referred to as the "not this" rune, Nauthiz presents a dynamic in which what is needed is what is resisted. We stand at a crossroads, from which vantage point we can see where to go, yet we don't move. Why?

When studying the history of Nauthiz the phrase "need fire" comes up. Reminiscent of the practice of thwarting malady by season-ally stepping through fire to be cleansed, the heart of such a cleansing practice is that we must be active participants in letting go of what hinders us. The only way to truly fill a need is to step in to the heart of what's missing. Hence its association with tension. To embrace what's missing we have to be willing to leap in to the faith and work of knowing that what we need will be there, without knowing what that is.

How we accept what we're resisting right now tells the tale. We have choices in the matter. It can go gracefully or drag us into a fiery pit of despair. At the bottom of every niggling anxiety lies a truth. It may be a very small truth, though it's a powerful one. At this time we must be willing to drag out all the self-help, mindfulness, and centering techniques we can to get to that little truth. That's the gold, and in the true sense of tension between extremes, it will set us free.

Nauthiz asks us to step into the cleansing fire and confront what most needs to be addressed in our lives. Meeting that need releases it, which is the ultimate significance of this stave. It brings very much a "fear itself" moment. Instead of fearing what's going to happen once in the fire, look to the relief of what the fire will alleviate.

If there's a charm to Nauthiz it's that we become so uncomfortable in its presence that we accept the change. We accept the need. We fulfill what it needs. We struggle until we've exhausted anything but right direction. I know it's not much comfort, but there's that.

If being dragged into despair flips the necessary switch, so be it. If it can be flipped without that, write the book. We'd all read it.

Remember, this stave can't be reversed. Allow its wisdom to be.

◆ DEVOTIONAL

When I was growing up my grandfather eliminated aggressive overgrowth and creepy crawlies by doing controlled burns in our yard. Armed with a torch and water hose, he'd section off an area to burn, then hose the scorched earth. He'd carefully seed, then tend it, until finally green life renewed. Then he'd move on to another section the next year.

Think back to the first moments of meeting your Shadow with Uruz. This was a pivotal shadow moment, which led you to a deeper experience of yourself. It led you to power.

Hold thoughts of a dynamic that needs to change in your life. It may be a health condition that needs addressing, a boundary that needs adjusting, a needed change in a relationship. Whatever it is, hold the feelings of it. How would you describe them? What memories do they conjure?

Now, remember the feelings of joy that Wunjo cultivated and invite them to sit alongside this need. What tension comes up in the urge to resist one or the other? With which do you feel the most comfort? Remember that you don't have to judge them. They don't have to be condemned or celebrated, only witnessed. Each brings valid information for you.

If you can imagine this need and joy as beings standing at opposites sides of a crossroads, with yourself in the middle, ask them to greet each other in the middle. How do they behave toward each other? How do you feel as you witness this interaction?

What action can you take in your everyday life to address this need?

You don't have to know what's going to grow back from the controlled burns of your life. For now it can be enough to know that you took action to remove what wasn't working and allowed need to be revealed.

Nauthiz Half-Month Affirmation

From the middle
I see myself
On all sides.

15
November 28–December 13
◆ Isa ◆
Excavating Hidden Life Force

Coming in to this cold time, Nauthiz forced us to face a deep personal truth, which in turn enabled us to meet some need. In the middle of the winter trio—Hagalaz, Nauthiz, Isa—and through the crossroads' discomfort, it motivates movement, which sets the stage for Isa.

Isa is the freeze that must happen before spring can return. It's the long, dark wintry sleep that must happen for what must die off to do so. Without that natural balancing of resources, what must be fed would starve. Isa, thus, is what must be fed.

Think about it: freezing has to happen for chaff to die off, for new life to have space, nutrients, and motivation to form, to grow. In Nature's cycle what comes from that seemingly restful creative state doesn't become apparent until the following spring. As plant and animal life hibernate and come back to life in warm weather, so do we. This is the cyclic trend of which Isa speaks, the necessity of the freeze.

Though it is the last of the winter staves, the result of what potential can come of facing and meeting the need of Nauthiz, Isa marks the beginning of another runic cycle. The progression of Isa (second ætt), Mannaz, then Ingwaz (both of the third ætt) will be one we revisit throughout seasons. It is the progression of the sacred seed into being.

Meaning "ice," Isa doesn't just portray a frozen state. It indicates the stuff of creation, the icy rime of Ginnungagap (the void) indicated in two of the books of the *Prose Edda,* Gylfaginning and Skáldskaparmál. Isa is the ice that formed Audhumla and Ymir. In this context ice isn't just solid water. It's the crystallization of the sacred seed, the heart of All Things distilled into the consciousness of every thing. It is new consciousness growing into its own life force.

As we've come through the creative process of the first ætt, we know this growth happens gradually, most certainly walk-don't-run energy. Indeed nourishment of the sacred seed can't be rushed. It is the epitome of trusting in right time, right place, right action. Nothing about this rune can be forced, coerced, or quelled. Remember that sitting still requires as much effort as motion. Such is the mantra of this half-month. As it can't be reversed, allow its process to unfold. While the urge may be to push forward, now isn't the time that such effort can be beneficial. In fact attempts to create large change at this time will result in conflict, which directly impedes the change. The current life force just isn't supportive of that kind of manifestation at this time.

All that's required now is to let the life force of this half-month bubble to the surface. Whatever it is we don't have to understand it. Even if it comes in with dazzlingly clear insight we don't have a green light to do anything with it—yet. Giving the process room and attentiveness to unfold in its own time is the emphasis for now.

◆ Devotional

In the heart of winter Isa sets in motion an evolution of events that culminates with Ingwaz in May. Such is the normal trajectory of the runic calendar. Apart from your usual runic observations of the season, take careful note of thoughts and feelings that come up at this time. Detail budding projects and new life dynamics.

Now is the time to assess skills in allowing the unrecognizable. Often when we have moments of vivid inspiration—deep unconscious rumblings that culminate in profound aha moments (as with Kenaz)—we're moved to allow them without impediment. However when we have those that aren't as clear, those that don't readily come with description, setting, details— we're less likely to permit them. In fact we're more likely to fight them. What we don't know of ourselves and fight is our Shadow. Isa guarantees an opportunity to tend the Shadow life force within us that over time will serve us well. We don't have to fear the guesswork of this one.

While its life force may be more obtuse, less identifiable, galdr Isa. Let it come in and reveal itself. Plan space to work with the feelings it brings up, the life dynamics it challenges. Although it isn't as obvious as the energy of other runes, the impact of Isa is intense.

Isa Half-Month Affirmation

I lie frozen, awake,
Sleeping only to dream
What comes next.

16
December 13–December 28
⋄ Jera and Yule ⋄
Finding Tools That Work

Yule is popularly observed between December 20 and 23 in the north, though its timing is based on the sun moving in to Capricorn. In the Southern Hemisphere it is widely celebrated between June 20 and 23. Encompassing Winter Solstice, this observation corresponds with honoring the dísir, or female ancestral spirits. For some, Yule marks the new seasonal cycle.

Jera, or "year," is the rune of inventory, or Hearth Accounting 101, as I call it. Historically this season brought midwinter, and it was necessary to know what provisions were at hand, how long they'd last, how many they would feed and warm, and what needed to be kept back to plan for the coming year. In this very practical time planning was essential, as was rationing.

Spiritually Jera comes at the point of a second wind. It's the reprieve before spring, to get things in order to plan for the next year. Indeed we look back at the year that has passed, though in hopes of applying that wisdom to better manage what comes. In this way we gain new tools, which at this corner of the Dark Time are ultimately the light we weren't expecting.

Jera is the realization that we don't have to do things alone. We can draw on past knowledge and experience, and we can apply that wisdom to our present condition (örlög), which can impact how we move forward (wyrd). It is the point along the hero's journey that we acquire sidekicks and allies to help us with that process.

Also, as we've seen with other runic relationships, Jera begins within the second ætt a micro-cycle that moves through Eihwaz and culminates with Perthro. How we manage Jera has direct impact on how we fare with the other two. How we deal with this micro-cycle sets us up for eventually moving on to the third ætt.

In the unfolding story of the runes Jera stands for the acquisition of tools, specifically of the ability to value personal experience and translate it into wisdom. Generally speaking Jera is all about the realization and activation of one's self as a guide, an informant in the Dream Team. At Jera's time in the sun, this is especially true.

Significant to the rune calendar is that Jera will always be the stave of Yule. This time of year will always be set aside for reviewing and restructuring, releasing and reassuring. Take this wisdom into the upcoming year and build observation of this natural reboot into end-of-year rituals. Indeed work the practical math of closing and opening, but also work in the spiritual rituals of ending and beginning, delving deeply into what must be grieved, blessed, loved, and planted.

◆ YULE INITIATION

To begin this initiation take ·time to realize your resources: your Dream Team support network, your skills. Bear in mind that this isn't a wish list. It isn't the support you wish you had but that which is readily evident and available to you. Consider the following, and take notes on each:

Who supports your dreams?
Who fosters your skills?
Who brings you up when you feel down?
Who helps care for your body?
Your mind?
Your soul?
How best do you learn?
In what location do you feel most connected?
What comforts you?

What encourages you?

What do you do best?

What life areas need attention?

Take some time to complete your list of resources and go back through it another time or two. After doing so jot down two or three goals you can accomplish in the next year. Again, these aren't wish-list items but actionable, doable outcomes. Make a schedule and plan for how they will be achieved, if needed. What's significant in this practical work is that you break it down. Realize who your help is, what parts of it are doable on your own, and what parts you need help with. Commit to engaging others and resources to reach these goals. If you sense hesitancy about acting on these goals, examine that closely.

When you feel solid about a direction with resources and goals, go to a quiet space and sing to them. Whatever words come, allow them. The sounds, melody, tone, galdr—let it move through you. Don't worry about what it says or how it sounds. The power crux of magick lies at the synthesis of inspiration and creation—spirit and form. There are many ways to celebrate that union, though we forget that our voice—spell-song moving through us into being—is one of the most potent. For this reason it's one of the most effective and powerful forces in childhood. Everything likes being sung to, even the resources that support you and the goals they help you to reach.

Sing to your allies regularly so that when you express need and reach out, they have strength upon which to stand for you.

Jera Half-Month Affirmation

Wisp of light
In the dark unknown—
Both are allies in my success.

17
December 28–January 13
⋄ Eihwaz ⋄
Navigating the Personal Path

The thirteenth rune in the traditionally accepted ordering of the Elder Futhark, Eihwaz indicates a death, or transformation, from which we can't turn. As with the four runes preceding Eihwaz, this rune can't be reversed.

Having come through Jera at Winter Solstice we have settled in to the realization that we don't have to do things alone. Jera is the acquisition of tools, perhaps allies, a means to implement plans for the coming year. Eihwaz brings a reality check of the double-edged sword variety. Knowing that we have helpful beings and resources to support us doesn't change the fact that we're alone no matter what and that self-power really is what sustains momentum. This stave marks the point in the natural order that we realize everyone else is merely an informant, for we remain our best resource. We can have all the spirit guides and tools possible, but the final decision to engage, to move, must come from ourselves.

Likewise Eihwaz teaches the fine balance of knowing where and when to turn to our resources and when and how we must sustain ourselves.

This rune demands that we come into close, regular dialogue with all aspects of self—the everyday get-the-dishes-done self, the Sacred Self, the body, mind, ego, life force. All that we perceive ourselves to be, and beyond that perception, is available as an ally. Must we know it all right away, right now? No, and that's not even a feasible expectation. However holding open the possibility that diverse components of the self can inform us on the best direction for the present dynamic is a wonderfully powerful skill to have.

If we contain all these facets of our own being that can bring useful insight to life concerns, why aren't they already doing it? Maybe they are, and we just don't know how to hear them. Or perhaps the onus remains on the earthly consciousness to ask, as the process of doing so grants us unconscious permission to stand in our power. It reawakens some spark of knowing that we are powerful.

Therein lies the relevance of Eihwaz. It arrives at the point of realizing that permission must be given and that radical change is afoot. Whatever corner presents itself, anticipate an ordeal when you turn it. But of course therein lies the key to managing Eihwaz. Translated as "yew," in the *Hávamál* it carries connotations of climbing a tree trunk, a metaphor of advancing into the transpersonal space for trance. It hearkens back to Odin's ordeal on the World Tree, which is a version of the trial in a shamanic journey—reconciling that point between life as we know it and beyond what we know of it. Approaching such paradoxes without warning is traumatic, certainly initiatory. Eihwaz brings the warning that such a transition is coming. When I have the choice between the ordeal I don't know and the ordeal I do know, I choose the latter, every time.

And of course ordeal has a specific connotation in the heathen tradition. It refers to initiations that lie beyond the ego barrier, and they're generally stressful if not painful. They require leaving the body behind, to explore what's needed at deeper levels.

At this time trauma is in the eye of the beholder. We don't often get to stand in our power on this one; we merely withstand. For this half-month we have an opportunity to realize radical change and go with it. The elements are at our disposal to do exactly that: to allow movement, to go forward, to breathe through change.

Eihwaz is the juncture of what happened in the past (ours and our ancestors) and how we behave now. In this juncture how we proceed through Eihwaz into the next half-month of Perthro becomes relevant, as does the relationship between the two runes.

In the second ætt comes Jera, Eihwaz, then Perthro. Having the house in order (Jera), we meet the End (Eihwaz). Then we drop everything, make peace with the fact that nothing crosses the white line but our bare selves, and progress to a clean start with wyrd (Perthro). When examined in that light there is a formula to how all of this works, and through the runic wheel progression we have a ritualistic opportunity to be ready for it.

◆ DEVOTIONAL

On the shamanic path, when we speak of initiation it means that we have an experience from which we can't return to life as the same person. In fact to attempt to do so creates more distress. However just because our vision or experience of ourselves has changed doesn't mean that we automatically have the life skills to know how to go forward.

Think back on the most transformational experiences of your life. Which was more challenging, the ordeal or coming back to everyday life afterward? How did you sort it all out?

When you think back to such experiences, how do they manifest in your body? Where do you feel them? How do your pulse and breathing respond to these memories?

How would you like to process such experiences differently moving forward?

Eihwaz Half-Month Affirmation

For initiation,
I risk who I am
To myself.

18
January 13–January 28
✦ Perthro ✦
Confronting Your Wyrd

This stave of completion and detachment brings nurture and calm for dealing with the unknown. It comes at the cold heart of winter and brings still contemplation.

We have come through the acquisition of allies and sat with knowing the ultimate choice in how to respond is always ours, alone. With that knowledge in hand we graduate to Perthro, which I call the "What do *you* think?" rune. The stave of feelings, Perthro is the moment we realize that it's all on us and we sink or swim by our own hand. Any issue we bear to it, any concern we raise for its insight, any dynamic wanting its influence, the response is the same—What do you think?

Perthro is the synergy of our past and our present in balance to create a sought-after outcome. Those of the new vernacular may consider it akin to the law of attraction, while old schoolers may consider it luck, though it's a more complete formula than either of those. In the traditional ordering of the Elder Futhark, successfully moving through Jera to Eihwaz produces solid ground for Perthro. It's the sure thing of efforts and embodiment manifesting the desired wyrd. These efforts include healing of ancestral lines, acceptance of what can't be changed from the past, and responding to both of these in a way in the present that brings it all into balance for the entire line, not just oneself. This is the ultimate culmination of Jera, Eihwaz, and Perthro.

What's nice is that this expression of the runic calendar will always offer this support this time of year. This progression through the last three months will always emphasize attentiveness to what we're creating and how we create it.

Perthro forces us to face our role in how wyrd plays out. It's not an accident, or something randomly thrown at us; neither is it a perfect formula we can dial up for a predictable outcome. It presents, however, a thorough collection of avenues we may address, heal, or engage to better position ourselves to manifest desires. This process is accomplished by reminding us that we are connected to All Things. Just as how others behaved before us affects our wyrd, so does how we behave affect our wyrd, that of those around us, and that of those who follow. Perthro is the rune of responsible manifestation. Through it we devote active participation in our outcomes, which is nothing less than attention to the past, balance brought to bear, and responsibility for present actions. Pretty straightforward, really, yet so very challenging to accomplish.

◆ DEVOTIONAL

When you roll dice you know what your options are. You can't predict what the outcome will be, though you know the exact parameters for what's possible. The same logic can be applied to our lives. However, coming into the knowledge of what the parameters are requires a great deal of awareness, and usually healing.

How comfortable are you with chance?

How comfortable are you with risk?

Take some time over this half-month to learn about your four cardinal family lines—mother's father and mother, father's father and mother. Most of us don't have to dig back too far to form a loose picture of what challenges they may have faced, what the joys and circumstances of their lives may have been. If you can go further back into the family lines, do, though it isn't required. Look to them to observe rather than analyze.

Likewise explore your own life with as much detachment as possible, as if you were standing apart from yourself, looking down over it. Note any specific events or experiences that stand out. As with relatives, this examination isn't about judgment or punishment but about coming into the fullest knowing possible about your path of manifestation.

What feelings from events or eras stand out in contrast to what you want in your life right now? Take careful note of these as well. What life areas move easily, and which do not?

When you've had the opening to sit with the information you've culled from looking back over your family and personal past, ask the aspect of you that manages your wyrd to meet you in a quiet space. In the Norse tradition this would have been called your *hamingja* (luck), though you should use the wording that best describes the part of All That You Are that oversees your ability to manifest your desires. In Old Norse culture luck wasn't the binary good or bad indicated in modern understandings; rather it was more along the lines of wyrd—your personal tapestry of past deeds, inner motivations, ancestral influences, and capability, all of which determine outcomes.

If you don't sense this part of you, begin singing to it, daily. Invite it. Create the space for it to come, and offer it prayers of healing. If you do this work daily there will be a response, a change that allows you to feel connected to this part of you, within a week.

As you sense this part of you, ask your Spirit Allies to bring the healing most needed to it. When you feel that healing has been carried through, ask for healing for yourself. At the culmination of this work, sit with this aspect of yourself. Go with what comes up, engage all senses, and observe how it feels to sit in proximity to your greatest potential.

Again, this isn't wish-list stuff. It's raw, duty-bound work on behalf of you and the many who came before. It is what is, and what lies ahead of you.

Take a few minutes to tell this part of you what you want and what your struggles have been in achieving it. Then ask it what it needs from you to feel movement for its desires and needs. Make the agreements necessary to support what this aspect of you needs, and thank it. Close the space.

You can revisit it, as needed.

You cannot and will not be able to change it all. The best we can do with much of the legacy we're handed and our own pasts is to own them.

In doing so we have no blinders to our potential, investment, or imagination. When we face this component of our wyrd, we gain the backbone to show up, which in itself opens many pathways.

Perthro Half-Month Affirmation

All we have been,
All that I am,
Is my duty to bear.

19
January 28–February 12
✦ Algiz and Imbolc ✦
Embodying Power

Imbolc is the time of light returning. Still chilled by the nip of winter we begin to see potential, to feel progress toward something beyond the immediate frozen moment. Celebrated in early February, Imbolc, or as this time would have been called in the Norse tradition, Disting, was a time of preparation. It was the point of stepping in to personal and communal power, having spent the isolated winter laying the basis from which to do so.

We've spent abundant time assessing and allocating for our needs, as well as coming in to deep awareness for how we can clear family lines and ourselves to make the best of what we have in the present. It makes sense that at this time in the season we'd look to protecting the resources and knowledge we've amassed.

Along with this time of readying the home space for the warmer season, Algiz arrives as a rune of protection, though it's not as simple as a white line drawn in the sand. Meaning "elk/sedge" this stave brings to mind that we are so connected to our home space, which, given the significance of the meaning of both *elk* and *sedge,* would imply we embody our Land Elders or Nature Spirits. Where Land Elders are humans who have across time agreed to stay bonded to a specific piece of land, Nature Spirits are the natural beings who inhabit it. They may be fae, animals, trees, elementals, totems, and so forth who share the land area with you.

They may function as allies, transient support, or indifferent neighbors.

Likewise we also have Home Spirits—guardians of our living space and the spirit of the rooms and dwelling itself. With strong animistic overtones the protection of this rune stems from not just being aware of the Home Spirits but being in concert with them as well, being in direct relationship with them. When we fully embody the spirits of home, they travel with us everywhere we go. In that light everywhere becomes home. The protection of that tribal bond travels with us, and it's the strongest magick there is. These beings are your immediate animistic community.

Indeed Algiz isn't a static line drawn in the sand. It's the deepest embodiment of place and its spirits—a boundary and weapon that goes with us everywhere.

◆ IMBOLC SABBAT INITIATION

First and foremost, nothing must be completed right this minute, or in the space of this half-month; rather consider this initiation a meeting, marking the beginning (or renewal) of a relationship to last for all of life.

If at all possible plan to do this initiation once at sunrise and again at sunset. It can be repeated any time, though the vantage points offered by those moments are particularly vivid, if not fragile.

For the opening to this initiation, leave pen and paper behind and plan to jot down notes later. Begin empty-handed and openhearted. Likewise focus your awareness through four senses, as described below.

From a safe outdoor space close to home, face sunrise. This is your starting point. Announce aloud your intention to greet the Land Elders and spirits of your yard (or whatever your defined land boundary is). Ask your guides and/or Higher Power to bring healing needed to these beings, then invite them to ally with you.

With eyes closed observe the sounds, smells, and sensations that greet you. If you're someone who picks up on ambient flavors, notice how the elements tastes. If it helps, cover your eyes to allow your other senses to engage more fully. What elements are you aware of? Stay in this place for several moments and observe the sensuality of the space around you.

Open your eyes, then proceed around your outdoor area, following the daily path of the sun. Pause, as you feel led, to take in the sensuality of the area, with your eyes closed. Progress around the land until you've come full circle to the place you started.

Then, with pen in hand, note your observations of the trek. What sounds stood out most? Which were subtle? What other sensual encounters commanded your attention? Jot down any significant qualities of the time during your circuit.

At sunset repeat the processional, beginning with facing the sunset, and working back around the area, walking in the direction opposite to the sun's path. Again, cover your eyes if it helps you to feel more present through your other senses.

Did the same observations stand out, sunrise to sunset? What was different about the two experiences?

For now, begin with the commonalities of the two outdoor experiences. Note what was evident in both processionals. From a safe spot indoors or out, imagine going back to the starting point and taking the walk again. How do the experiences that stood out to you manifest in this liminal space? Can you engage them? If so, for now, express gratitude to these beings and reiterate your invitation to be family. Consider these beings the ones most available for direct relationship, at present, and repeat your invitation to them daily. When possible, take time to walk through your land and to do the follow-up imaginal walk. Also create a shrine, altar, or some offering to the Land Spirits. This could as simple as a bowl of water that you offer with intention to them, birdseed, or a song. However you honor them, do so safely, and tend the space regularly.

In the second week of this half-month, after you feel more direct connection with the Land Elders and Nature Spirits, bring your focus to the guardians of your home, the spirit of each room, and of the living space as a whole. Again, choose a starting point in your home. As before, announce yourself. For your living space, it's appropriate to ask for any beings who no longer need to be in your space to be moved on by your guides and to request that any guardians who do need to be in your space, come. Request healing for all of the above, including people who dwell there. Speak your invitation to live as a community to your Home Spirits. Proceed through each room with the same intention as outdoors. When you've finished moving through each room, take notes on your observations.

When you're ready, and just as you greeted the outdoor spirits, imagine walking from the starting room of your home and take the walk through again. As you approach areas that held a particular feeling or focus, observe how that life force now takes shape to you. Engage each as you can, and restate your intention for relationship with the space. Ask what it needs, and state your needs. In this way create an alliance with the spirits of your home and invite them to do exactly the same. As with the outdoor exploration, take a few moments to greet Home Spirits, daily. It doesn't have to be a long, involved ritual; rather it can be just a few seconds to honor them. By the end of this half-month, you will feel them reaching back.

As you become more acquainted with the spirits where you live—inside and out—begin exploring the parts of your space that you inherently embody and how they support you. When you're away from home, imagine walking back through the parts of your space where you feel most connected to them. Notice changes in how you feel in foreign spaces when you focus on your allies at home.

And of course, examine how you are consensually engaging in this same practice with the people who share these spaces with you.

Algiz Half-Month Affirmation

All under my sun,
All that I am,
Travels with me.

20
February 12–February 27
✦ Sowilo ✦
Remembering Infinite Divinity

The challenges of the second ætt are more physical, external, earthy—and we've risen to them through this winter season. Over this final half-month with this rune family we find the opportunity to wrap up that part of the journey and gain some steam for what comes next, of course without knowing exactly what that will be.

To help with that mystery, Sowilu reminds us of our place in divinity. It is the pay-it-forward stave, a state of charity with which most of us are familiar, if not exactly comfortable. Having gained a strong self through the year we are now fit to do something with it. However, while we're cozy with acts of divinity, often we aren't comfortable attributing divinity—being divine—to ourselves, particularly if our past revolved around the idea that such a state was unattainable by humans. We've been taught that only gods and goddesses are divine, and it's not an option for us. To think that we are divine plucks chords that may irritate past wiring. Now's the time to update.

Sowilu reminds us that divinity isn't something that happens to us but *through* us. It isn't above us, and we aren't below it. We're part of it; we *are* it. In that light responsibility shines through this "sun" stave. Once we realize that we're divine we're then called to some action. Thus the imagery I like for Sowilu is "The light that shines on us, so that we may shine on others."

By the time we encounter this closing rune of the second ætt, we've mastered the physical level of being. In the first ætt we worked through awareness of ourselves as thoughtforms and brought ourselves into being. In the second we have through baptism by fire committed to the challenges that being in form entails. Sowilu comes as the realization that we've accomplished that and can take a small break. Every ætt-closing stave comes with degrees of acknowledgment of what has passed, what is, and a sense of closure.

Yes, we're part of the divine process, yet we have our own plans, our own role. In carrying out that role Sowilu suggests that we sit for a spell and come into that knowledge, without necessarily making plans for what should be done with it.

◆ DEVOTIONAL

Cosmology is the narrative of creation. For some it is about literal science, for others it's an interpretation of that science. For some, it's both. Spend some time sussing out your cosmology and your relationship to it. When we feel a connection to how we—and perhaps everything—came into being, we understand better how to engage while here.

Consider what role divinity plays in your understanding of cosmology. What does it mean to you? How do you experience it in your life?

How comfortable are you with believing that you are divine? How comfortable are you believing in the divinity of others? If tension arises around these thoughts, sit with that tension through this half-month.

Sowilu is an inspiration rune. It helps us to realize that we're not alone and that we can be active in helping others know that as well.

> ### Sowilo Half-Month Affirmation
>
> All Things,
> Through you
> I am.

21
February 27–March 14
◆ Tiwaz ◆
Holding Space

This stave begins the third ætt, after the bright blessing and brief reprieve of Sowilu. We are two-thirds of the way through the runic year, coming upon spring. Now is the time of ripping out the roots of what's died and pruning back everything that has lain dormant. In Old Norse timing now sets the stage for the productivity we dreamed through the fall and winter (first and second ætt), of what will feed us over the year to come. It is the time of synthesizing our thoughtforms into action.

If that sounds familiar, it is. The first ætt dealt with a sense of first realizing our mysterious souls bore duties in form. We progressed from being thoughtforms, ourselves, into formed being. As we start this new era we are again confronting our power, responsibilities, and potential as creators, now from the vantage point of wisdom and knowledge. Strictly speaking, the third ætt focuses on our ability to hold on to our role in divinity throughout the mundane—in spite of the mundane. It also begins the final stretch of the year's initiations.

Each beginning and ending of the ættir brings a sense of between-space, a truly new territory between comfort in what is known and a gripping realization of the unknown. The hardest part of moving between ættir is coping with the feelings about doing it all over again. Don't be surprised if such feelings pop up over this half-month. Whether they come with shame, guilt, or sentimental soreness, realize that this is the cycle of all things in form. It's not indicative of a failure of healing, learning, or growth. This is the flow of life, here. It is as it should be.

I call Tiwaz the survivor rune as it's related to a change in battle plans, the assumption being that the battle is already afoot. It draws on survivor depths, then demands that we respond from that same depth. This isn't new drama; no shocker there. What comes as a surprise though is that the plan must change. Plan A will not work in the current dynamic, and it must be abandoned mid-confrontation. There's no gentle insinuation for an alternative strategy, no subtle reprieve to allow for regrouping. Also there's no time to strategize. It's game on, and roll with it as it comes. The challenge is remembering this info in the midst of the challenge.

With Tiwaz resistance to that change is what generates distress. Indeed change ripples out alarm. In the heat of battle realizing that the current plan isn't working and refusing to change it is what causes fatality. The ability to release Plan A and let it be dead is the key. Hence we have the skills to manage Tiwaz drama, we just didn't realize we had them.

Most people get upset when they find Tiwaz in a cast, because it insists upon self-directed unexpected change. The thing is, Plan B is victorious. The sooner onto that page, the more quickly success can roll in.

The reasons that we cling to Plan A are telling. Many of us cling to the safety of failure because we are afraid of success we can't imagine. We're afraid of change, even when what we have isn't serving us. A deeper current of this hesitation is grief. More than an inability to let go of the plan, we can't stop grieving its loss. Plan A was our heart's desire, our dream song. We wanted it with every fiber of our being. Letting it go is a death, of sorts. In many ways Tiwaz is concerned with the grief that comes when idealism has been stripped away. It isn't suggesting that the ideals can't be manifest; it's just not in the way we had in mind.

In this half-month an alarm button is hit, and the din telling us to run is real. Do not take the elevator. Invite the legwork of the stairs and let the alternate plan that's been brewing bloom into consciousness. It's the one. This avenue opens to a totally new terrain, with all new possibilities.

Tiwaz begins the third ætt, which above all points to an upswing in life force, an optimistic perspective, and the energy to follow through. The productivity of all our work is coming. We've done that legwork. The challenge is staying flexible to how it manifests, being clear enough to see it for what it is, and deft enough to foster what it needs—even if fostering doesn't look the way we thought it would.

◆ DEVOTIONAL

For this devotional consider how you remain aware of your spiritual self through the everyday. What small, brief daily practices do you do to remind you of your divinity? Where Sowilu fosters our realization that we are divine, Tiwaz challenges us to remember that divinity during adversity. It's easy to feel a sense of who you are at deeper levels when everything is fine, when you feel aligned and in tune, and your rewards meet your demands. When our heart song is not shaping up the way we've planned, remembering our divine connection and its power is not only difficult to do, but we tend to turn on ourselves and become our own enemy.

Use this half-month to revisit your relationship to divinity and learn how to carry it through daily acts. Now is the time that Nature has set aside for you to work out any tension or friction about things that stand in your way. It's likely time for a new plan; at minimum, time to regroup.

The concept of sacred space hinges on the belief and/or experience that intention focuses power. In fact sacred space could be considered intentional space. You are sacred space. Your ability to believe that has everything to do with your ability to believe you are divine.

Tiwaz Half-Month Affirmation

Who I am
Is sacred
Everywhere.

22
March 14–March 30
✦ Berkano and Ostara ✦
Healing Dues

Tiwaz brought a sense of action to be taken amid a dire need for change. Indeed all has hushed, considering the tumultuous start to the year and the boisterous winding down of winter. As we near the northern Vernal Equinox energies shift from the heaviness of winter to the busyness of spring. This equal time of day and night gives us a last opportunity to bask in stillness before the busy growth season comes. Where Imbolc heralded light's return, with Ostara it arrives.

The Vernal Equinox is one of two points in the year that light and darkness are virtually equal, which happens as the sun crosses the equator. That crossing brings a sense of pause, which is appropriate to the energy of Berkano.

Significant about the transition from Tiwaz to Berkano is this battlefield imagery. Where Tiwaz indicates an aggrieved change of plans mid-battle, Berkano soothes resulting friction. Telling though—it only soothes after the transition to Plan B has been accepted. We're forced to come to grips with loss before comfort can come. At least in this case comfort doesn't bring acceptance.

Keep in mind that purely from the standpoint of the runic calendar Berkano's arrival at the close of winter isn't an accident. Berkano is considered the midwifing rune in that it has overseen a significant project come to fruition and maintains the emotional detachment from it needed to let it take its own course. While it brings balm necessary to recover from battle, it doesn't force a healing process or plunge headlong into another fight. It offers no emotional attachment that would urge us to fight, flee, or freeze. We allow. We honor. We bless.

Berkano is a holding place, though not a forced one like the runes of the winter trio. It's a reprieve and a time to honor a job well done. For this half-month honor what's recently come to a close, without rushing into new projects; rather our task is to behold the creative space of rest. Berkano honors us, recognizes how hard we've worked, forces us to be present, and expects us to give props to ourselves. In the greater story of what's playing out this half-month, Berkano sustains us in needed soul searching.

◆ OSTARA SABBAT INITIATION

We aren't part of a culture that focuses on healing; rather we focus on results, which if you've ever been hurt or traumatized means that we often skip the real messy, dirty work of the healing process. In other words, we avoid pain and grief at all costs. Yet healing only comes through them, not instead of them. Ostara, or the Vernal Equinox, represents a time of natural healing. It is the season of building, birthing, and becoming. While the name Ostara comes from the Germanic goddess, Ēostre, little is known about how the Old Norse tradition observed the Vernal Equinox. In contemporary Northern Tradition observances fertility goddess Freya and the goddess of immortality, Idun, are honored.

Known for its soothing abilities, Berkano is the rune of Ostara. Most relevant with Berkano is the feeling of dues paid, the sense that what we've done is enough, even if all the ends aren't neatly tied up. Therein lies another key concern in Western culture. We assume that for something to reach a plateau of stability means that we're done with it forever. It's healed. It's finished. Few things are ever completely done, and Berkano urges us to cultivate a sense of realizing the plateaus that occur in the journey, without projecting what they should mean. Just find them. Just allow them. Realize the completion, without fretting, and for the moment, let it be. Indeed the ability to let things be is healing on its own.

To build, we must recognize what we have built. We must recognize the resources we have. To prepare for this Ostara initiation, list every life accomplishment—every one of them. Go into as much detail as needed to commit to paper how significant and profound each accomplishment was. Whether it's surviving childhood, graduating high school, developing a winning strategy for coping with depression, or crossing a trip to Ireland off the bucket list, reserve judgment or self-editing—just list the deeds.

When you've listed them, let the list sit a couple of days, then plan dedicated time to sit with each item. Depending on your list, this may take an hour or two.

In a quiet space, begin with the first item on the list, and thank it for showing up in your life. Thank it for every sense of pride and accomplishment it brought. Thank it for the wisdom and experience that blesses you still. Allow any exchange that needs to happen between the spirit of this item and yourself.

Thank All That You Are for the fortitude, resources, and sacrifices you made. If you had to make choices you're not proud of, so that you could be who you are today, bless them. Thank them. Allow permission for any tension around them to leave.

When you've gone through the list, take a few seconds to engage your body and feelings. This is what it feels like to sit in the presence of Ostara. This is what it feels like to be Berkano. Having felt it across your experience and in your form, you can now call on this feeling anytime you need. What's most significant about understanding your accomplishments is observing how many of them you don't remember. It's too easy not to remember how hard you worked. When we don't remember the effort we put into a wanted outcome, we forget how much effort it takes to keep going, to sustain manifestation of what we want and need. When we remember that effort, we retain the spirit that drives it all, and always did.

Call on this spirit during the time of Ostara, then draft another list. This time note what you want to accomplish now, with this auspicious season of building and creating in your favor. Be specific. Be detailed.

When the list is complete, take a few minutes outside and state to the Nature Spirits of your space—the domain of Ostara—what you need to fulfill the items on your list. When you've stated them clearly, ask that the needs be met.

Berkano Half-Month Affirmation

I did this.
I am enough.
I am enough.

23
March 30–April 14
✦ Ehwaz ✦
Meeting Allies

The holding pattern of Berkano brought balm and a sense of personal stability to the mix. We've come through glorious though draining toil and have tended the wounds from our efforts. Now's the time to get the house in order.

The rune Ehwaz tells us the effort we've put in up to this point will no longer be enough. It doesn't mean the way we've been doing it was wrong or fruitless; rather it calls us to take what we've been doing to the next level, and by next level I mean deeper. The subtlety of this stave is its power. It doesn't call for a grand overhaul of effort, just that it be finely focused at all levels of being.

This "horse" rune carries distinct shamanic overtones in that in Old Norse culture the horse carried soul seekers into ecstatic trance— or journeying, if you will. Discussion around this rune often gets stalled at "horse" and "journey," leaving its meaning to be along the lines of Raidho and "travel." However as those who have forayed into ecstatic trance know, it's not the ability to go into trance that makes it powerful. What's done with the information gained from trance, how it's manifest in waking, is what's critical. In that light Ehwaz is about boots-on-the-ground animism: living the Sacred Self, out loud.

Ehwaz tells us plainly that we are responsible for planting the seeds at all levels. All the elbow grease and brute force in the Multiverse isn't going to bring anything into being right now. What's called for is the full package of force (Fehu/action) and embodiment (Uruz/being), which means do the work, then make the work everything we speak, think, and dream. Become it. The words spoken must reflect the reality desired. The thoughts fostered must support what we say we want. Our daydreams must encompass a thoroughly choreographed stage of what is to be.

Likewise those who weave wyrd (as this process may be called) know, it can't all be selfish projection on our part. As we embody what we want in our lives we must also imagine a world that can support it. If it was as simple as interjecting what we want into being, we'd all have winning lottery tickets. The background, scenery, and soundtrack of that reality have to be as big as we can dream them. We embody not only what we want and need for ourselves but also how it will bless the being of All Things. We bring to bear our dreams by also imagining a world that can sustain them, can benefit from them, and that recognizes the dreaming itself.

Such is the collective component of blessing that needs to become daily practice. To create the things we want we must work to create the world that can realize them. For whatever we dream for ourselves, we must hold space for every being who also dreams this to be able to manifest it.

This is the crux of Ehwaz's reminder to dig deeper. Whatever is needed will not be found at superficial levels of being, and that new vantage point isn't just going to dawn on us. We have to set aside time, set the intention to delve into it, cultivate the life force to go there, then sustain the fortitude to see it through.

Ehwaz presents another midpoint along the greater progression of futhark initiation. We've begun the process and have some instinct about where it needs to go, how things should end up. Yet once in the guts of it we become disenchanted or afraid. We realize that we're in over our heads, because that's what initiation is. It's the invitation to go deeper than we ever imagined possible. However to become initiated we must complete the process. Otherwise we're just post-traumatic.

This half-month presents a turning point: Do we stagnate or soar?

◆ *DEVOTIONAL*

The most significant resource along any path of direct revelation is the acquisition of allies. We honored our practical allies with Jera, learning who to turn to for what need, and gaining the conviction to actually express that need and reach out. Ehwaz requires us to acquire not just what we think of as spirit helpers, guides, or soul guardians but also the ability to realize All Things at its source, that we are part of it. What we do matters, to All.

In part I of this book Ehwaz was associated with Sleipnir, Odin's horse, which carried him on his ecstatic ride through the World Tree. Such is the depth of the experience this rune brings. It is very much associated with ordeal initiation—suppression of the ego so that the soul awareness most needed can express itself. For this reason Ehwaz heralds a time of spiritual movement, over which we can have some control.

Drawing on the early work with Fehu and Uruz, with the Sacred Self and Shadow, ask them to share a quiet space with you. Check in with them if you haven't in a bit, and engage them until their familiarity enhances your peaceful space.

With their support ask for the Nature Being best suited to facilitate movement in a stuck life area to come. If it helps, name the area, though it's okay to keep it general. Go with the first impression, the first sense of what comes.

Engaging Nature Spirits can be awkward. The rune Ehwaz, in itself, can be helpful in smoothing out communications or interactions with an unfamiliar species. Also, don't overtax this first meeting. Express gratitude for the response to your inquiry, and ask what you can do for this ally. Ask what it needs. Let the interaction go as far as it will, then thank all in attendance.

As you progress through this half-month, devote daily time to meeting with this Nature ally. Allow the dialogue to develop with each visit. As well, make an offering to your immediate Nature space in honor of this ally. In this way you strengthen the ties between your power in other worlds and this one.

Ehwaz Half-Month Affirmation

Wherever I travel
I am consistent,
And ever changed.

24
April 14–April 29
◆ Mannaz ◆
Finding Your Tribe

Still smoothing the rough edges of the Ostara initiation initiation and coming into its wisdom through the intensity of Ehwaz, we're met with a relatively quiet time. Our focus has shifted from that deep, animistic observance of our latest initiation to a communal expression of what we took from it. Mannaz enters at a point where we have gained a new perspective and, to fully develop it, we must engage others— specifically others with whom we don't already have common ground or interaction. The idea is that we have this new life, this new consciousness in our hands, and to do the best we can with it we must educate ourselves. We must begin bringing it to the world. It's logical that as the season warms we seek social outlets that get us outdoors and moving. However the challenge of Mannaz is bringing something cherished to people we don't know and dealing with the insecurities and fears that may be part of that. In the biblical sense of the prophet never being known to his own people, so our brilliance through Mannaz goes invalidated by people who know us too intimately. They can't separate their emotional attachment to us from their reaction to our new consciousness. We need outside approval as well as feedback. All enlightenment is profound and intoxicating when we're marveling at it, sitting home alone. When we must bring it into the light and live its experience openly, our resolve to sustain the wisdom of that initiation is truly tested. New habits must be practiced consistently and regularly, or else they are lost. Now is that tender time of anchoring the change that becomes the new way. This foray doesn't have to be and shouldn't be done alone. As I've said before: we don't heal in isolation but in community.

The curious caveat of Mannaz is this business of its shiny newness. Given the recent ordeal, we're not likely to be met by established community. We're lucky if we are. We've gone through a process that left us radically changed, unable to greet the world as before, unable to be in the world as we were before. We need to find new minds, new thoughts, get new takes on this recently given awareness, and new support to help us take it further.

Ideally Ehwaz gave us the needed time to process this need so that we've developed perspective, possibly direction, and met it as a spiritual being. For those who could take the process to that depth this half-month clarifies direction and provides a tribe of new people to take things even deeper. New directions and possibilities open.

For those who didn't feel closure from the last couple of months the narrative of this half-month is a bit different. More akin to the experience of having gone on a fabulous but strenuous hike over high hills and into low valleys, taking in the beauty, awe, fatigue, interconnection, and then trekking back to the stasis of everyday. With only a few minutes to catch a breath we're asked to share the experience of this hike with others. Muscles aren't rested, cells aren't rehydrated. We may not have even bathed. We *want* to share it. The hike was gorgeous, replenishing, possibly even life-altering. Yet—it *just* happened. We don't totally understand it all, and we're being called to find meaning in it, then situate it in some common space with others. That can be quite an uncomfortable dynamic. What if people don't get it? What if they say it's wrong? What if they encourage us to try yoga instead? What if they don't care?

To know what we know we must take that awareness into new places, among new people. As long as we keep it to ourselves it can only aspire to be escapist or precious. When we can hold it amid diversity it becomes true wisdom. Fortunately Mannaz carries with it a general positive support for just that. Because now is its native time of season, the new forces we need to develop and grow our wisdom are available.

Another facet of Mannaz's "coming out" significance stretches way back to Isa. Recall that Isa, meaning "ice," is the final rune of the winter trio. It represents the sacred seed just below the surface. More specifically, it is the frozen Niflheimr principle of the Old Norse creation story. In that light Isa is eternal. It is the part of All Things that is both indestructible and always coming into being. While all these other, obvious initiations and cycles have been playing out across the Elder Futhark, this sacred seed has been growing, thriving, getting ready to burst into life. With Mannaz it exerts its need for atmospheric support.

We are each responsible in our own way for engaging that process and bringing our unique gift to sustain its calling. Part of our role in tending that calling is making sure the seed has everything it needs. The challenge in giving it what it needs is putting ourselves in the position to experience new things and gather support. We know we can give it what we have, specifically what we have in excess. We must learn what else it needs, though doing so can be a triggering maneuver for folks comfy in their ruts. Taking the initiative to step into new spaces and engage new places and new people is likely not going to be comfortable. However, without doing so, the seed can't reach its apex of growth with upcoming Ingwaz.

Metaphorically speaking that sacred seed is new thought, new consciousness. The micro-cycle playing out since Isa is one in which we've been asked to change our minds about something and to allow the support to come in to foster that change. The main goal on our end is not to get in the way of that process. In fact nothing else can get in the way of it at this time.

For this half-month we get to not just see but to create the big shift we need. We get to look back and see the foundation we've built for it so that we can be present to the process of taking it further, deeper. Give it time, space, and nurture to root. Find a team of support that can help with that. No looking ahead; rather indulge vigilant tending of personal needs and forget the rest for now.

◆ DEVOTIONAL

Unless you're a confident, happy extrovert, the memo to get out into new social groups is a challenging one. Even if you are that extrovert, waving your new freak flag still isn't easy in a group of strangers.

Make the effort to find targeted support for what has transpired from recent initiations. Search for groups related to your need or subject. Seek out peers and a mentor who can help you hone your skills. If this new consciousness presents as needing to learn how develop your relationship to herbs, take a horticulture or gardening class. If you are a gifted dream interpreter, find a forum that allows you to practice your skills. The ability to bring it forward into community now ensures its ability to grow into a lasting, changed life view. The rawness of it may make such outreach feel like too big of a stretch. The glory of it is that Mannaz is the tone of the season. It's in our favor to find that new community. You still must look for it however. It won't just come to you.

What self-clarity have you gained over the course of working with the runic calendar? Having come to know deeper aspects of self with the first ætt, your Dream Team of support with Jera, and Spirit Allies with Ehwaz, what new community is worthy of your revelations? What do you need to learn to better support them? What skills or training are needed? What witness or mentor will help you take it further?

What knowledge, wisdom, and resources will you act on to find the tribe you need?

Mannaz Half-Month Affirmation

Whoever I am,
Whoever shows up,
Is wholly me.

25
April 29–May 14
✦ Laguz and Beltane ✦
Staying in Flow

Beltane is the cross-quarter sabbat that indicates the halfway point between Vernal Equinox and Summer Solstice. Some celebrate it May 1, while others observe it at 15 degrees of Taurus. We've fully moved from the sterile elements of winter into the fertile grounds of summer.

In the Celtic tradition Beltane is called May Day, though on the Old Norse Path it's known as Walpurgis, a nine-day festival culminating with Walpurgisnacht. This sabbat honors Odin's sacrifice on Yggdrasil to bring the runes into human consciousness, demonstrated through the Wild Hunt, or ritualistic confrontation of Shadow through the ninth night endeavor with the spirits of the forest and Ancestors.

Because this is the natural position of Laguz on the calendar it's even more integral that we take the time to connect with the forces of support available to us. What we plant now is what grows for the rest of the year.

Where Ostara is the time of light's arrival, Beltane is what grows from its warmth.

The half-month stave Laguz brings a time that we could flow naturally with elemental currents. We don't have to feel that we're carrying the load ourselves or that there's too much to carry. I say "could," as it's our choice to recognize that help is there and to allow it to support us.

If we can't slow down and take a minute to realize that we could be in the flow, the flow may as well not even be there.

Laguz continues to facilitate our progress through those jagged edges and into a space that we can better be carried by resources available to us. This stave challenges us to realize the places where we're able to move with the current, where we resist it, and where we completely lose touch with all of the above. Such observation and adaptation is the hardest part to learn to weave wyrd. We must sustain some awareness of how we're engaging the elements around us. Even if we're not very good at engaging them, staying in touch with how we're engaging them is what counts. The more we become aware of that connection, the better we get at actively participating in it.

Should autopilot drift in, turn it off and reengage. Begin again. The thing is, we know what feels right and what doesn't. The deeper challenge is to stay in that awareness. It's much easier to just shrug it all off and not notice, because once noticed, discomfort must be dealt with. As Beltane indicates the season of what can grow, Laguz symbolizes the inherent life force that fosters growth.

◆ Beltane Sabbat Initiation

I have a bodyworker friend who has always told me that our relationship to water is the most significant elemental bond humans have; as adults we are 55 to 60 percent water. It is our foremost elemental connection to everything in this realm. To honor it fully without, we must first honor it within.

At Imbolc the initiation brought deeper acquaintance with Home Spirits—the Nature and space allies that protect, grow, and live with you. Much as you found common roots with them, so with the watery ways of Beltane do you find greater interconnection.

All connection begins where you stand. There is no other place for it to begin. All the New Age teachings that project you out of your body and beyond your ego awareness strip you of vital grounding that would otherwise allow you to anchor star-studded wisdom in boots on the ground. With Laguz you can't skip your body's experience of water or you will perish. You can't skip your soul's experience of water, for then you won't be able to recognize when you are carried by flow.

Your body is beautiful. Your ego is primed. Both are functioning exactly as intended, together. While they do so you can explore that there is still more of you to access. In fact there is more of you beyond you to access, and you don't have to forsake the earthly parts of you to get to it. You shouldn't forsake them to get to it, or you won't be able to hold what you gain.

Find a quiet, undisturbed spot outdoors in your living area. Close your eyes, and come into the imaginal experience of this place as you did in the final part of the Imbolc initiation. Invite the spirits of the space to stand with you on the periphery of this initiation.

When you've greeted them and addressed any needs they may present, honor all the beings of the space, even those you've not personally encountered. Then ask specifically for the water of the space to come. Water above ground, in the sky, in you, in the plants and trees, beneath the rocks—all of it. Allow it time and space to stand with you and observe its nuances. Are there different kinds of water, sourcing from different components of the land, sky, or experience? If so, is there a collective aspect— beyond being water—each shares? What does each have in common?

As you become aware of that focal point, find where it resides in the water within you. Notice how it feels and what senses it stirs. How does it flow through your body?

When you feel a connection to how it maps in your form, explore the points where the water in you joins with the water of the space around you. How does it flow? Does the mapping of your body change as you stretch beyond its boundaries? Does your experience of water change as that within you connects to the water around you?

Sit with that expanded sense of self through water as long as it's comfortable. Explore any aspects of it that intrigue you. If you feel ready, further widen your experience of self through water. How does your experience of being the water of the space stream into the water of the wider region around you? Again, note any changes in body flow, awareness, movement.

Hold the wider experience of being water. Sing to it. Chant the galdr of Laguz. As you become aware of its boundaries and potential, thank it for what it brings to your life and your living space, your town, your region. When you're ready to return to your waking experience of the space, come back to the water of your region, then the water of your outdoor area, then finally the water of your body. Open your eyes.

The potential to experience the extremes and depths of water through yourself is limitless. You can take it far as land boundaries, oceans, the planet.

Of course you don't have to, because knowing what flow feels like is enough. Knowing you are part of it at any level, at the level you feel called to act in, is precisely right for you.

Laguz Half-Month Affirmation

I am this.
I am you.
We are.

26
May 14–May 29
◆ Ingwaz ◆

Feeding New Consciousness

As we slide deeper into summer we become aware of how what we've planted is beginning to grow. Our time with Ingwaz is a precious yet hard-won gift. It's the sacred seed of Isa, forged by Mannaz, in the palm of our hand. These three runes deal directly in the shaping of new consciousness.

Think back to our time with Isa, which would have been the close of last year, specifically mid-November through mid-December. What began then as an idea or newly turned dynamic at that time—a potential—is coming or has come to fruition now. Isa, the third of the winter trio, holds the blueprint of our work for the year.

Also look at the events playing out during Mannaz, which was mid to late April. The most profound things in our lives don't grow in the expected places or with rote care. They demand new life force, demand that we change, which is Mannaz. What began with Isa took a significant turn in our favor for control during Mannaz. We came into resources or support that prior to that wasn't available. Where Isa is the sacred seed, Mannaz is the new tribe or conditions to foster it.

Other factors in the meaning and application of Ingwaz come from the Elder Futhark and the Younger Futharks. In the Elder Futhark, the origin of them all, Ingwaz is represented by a squatty diamond shape.

In this depiction its semblance as a seed is more evident. The emphasis on the space contained within it is the focus. In the Anglo-Saxon Futhark it is drawn as two Gebos stacked atop each other. The focus space in the middle is still there, though the strokes supporting it are omitted. What's interesting about this depiction and why it has bearing on how the rune can be translated requires reflecting on the meaning of Gebo. Partnership is what's generally attributed to Gebo, the ultimate gift. However when Ingwaz is considered to be two stacked Gebos, the meaning refines more closely to "as above, so below," the real ultimate partnership. Between those two, miraculous things happen—in that focused, sacred center.

If we start with Isa (second ætt) as the sacred seed encased in the safety of ice, this state of suspended thoughtform preparing to burst into being is one component of the crux of Old Norse creation (the other factor in that equation is fire, some say Fehu, which stimulates the sacred seed into action, from the ice). As the sacred seed is part of everything, it is part of us as well. It is a critical component of how we create ourselves going forward.

Tiwaz brings the point that our sacredness is challenged in some way, externally, which signals the need for internal revolution. Tiwaz is associated with Tyr and Tuisto, each a god or leader (one and the same) who under duress realized that he couldn't save his people. However metaphoric or literal, the analogy here ties into deep grief, the realization while in the trenches that the only way through that grief is to feel it fully, set life up so that process can happen regardless of the trenches, and do it fully. Hence we have Tiwaz's warrior connotations.

Tyr saved his people through his son, Mannus, or Mannaz. Recall a few weeks ago, we visited Mannaz as the point that we had to take our new awareness out for a spin. We were challenged to bear the results of germinating that sacred seed and moving through the grief of what that means in human terms and show our gooey insides to other people.

Ouch.

Yet that's where the story dramatically improves. Isn't it always? Through sharing the plight of his grief and loss of his people with

Mannus, Tyr saw the three tribes that made up Bronze Age Germania: the Herminones, Istaevones, and Ingaevones. The Ingaevones, or Ingwaz, represent that bright shiny new consciousness birthed. It is the sacred seed in form. It is the culmination of everything that seed went through, every thought and feeling it had about that process, the receptacle of what everyone else thought about that process, the wounds, scars, strengths, and power of its every step in to being.

It's the story of us all.

It's the story of what we do here, and why we do it.

It's the revelation of calling and the drive to serve.

Who we truly are is best glimpsed right now. Anything not feeling quite on, get a plan laid out for how to wholly, compassionately rerail it, and make it happen. Adore every bit of what's revealed—even the difficult, challenging bits—because we worked our asses off to get here. There's no big ritualistic finish, no searing brand to stamp the job complete. It's complete, for now. Let it be. Hold it and self delicately and tell it every wonderful thing you adore about it—directly in the mirror. Allow this moment to be, because the progression continues on to another initiation shortly. Now is the time to bring closure to this one.

◆ DEVOTIONAL

Truly, when is the last time you said something kind to yourself in the mirror? When is the last time you lavished praise upon yourself, in the mirror? Take some time during this half-month to do exactly that, and note how it feels. What thoughts or memories come up as you look into the mirror and speak? Do the same feelings come up each time you look into the mirror and address yourself? How do they change?

Having spent some focused time with yourself, consider who you bring to the world. Is it the person in the mirror? How are you getting support for *that* you? What is it that you are bringing to the world? What service does it offer?

Also during this half-month, take some time to track the path of the life currents that arose with Isa (November–December), progressed through Mannaz (April), and have now arrived at Ingwaz. One of the hardest parts of manifestation is recalling what worked and what didn't. Now is the time to document that process and fine-tune it for next year.

> ### *Ingwaz Half-Month Affirmation*
> Everything I've worked for
> Is now, is coming,
> Will be.

27
May 29–June 14
✦ Othala ✦
Being the Present

We spent the past half-month with Ingwaz teaching us who we are and how we bring that person to the world. Moving into Othala, we're asked to deepen that to a perspective of service and to see it as a legacy. Most interpret this stave simply as "inheritance," and indeed it does tap into matters of one's estate, having affairs in order, and being aware of lineage. From a shamanic standpoint it asks that we turn to the Ancestors.

If you recall from part 1, Othala is usually indicated as the last stave in the Elder Futhark. However, in the calendar, Dagaz is the last. The reversal of these runes isn't unheard of. In fact among the oldest complete renderings of the futhark are the Vadstena and Mariedamm bracteates (dating from 500 CE), which show Dagaz as the final stave. Compelling arguments are made for both placements, though for the runic calendar Dagaz occurs last. Dagaz, and thus Summer Solstice, portend a drastic ending, followed by the obliteration of extremes. For this reason it stands exactly opposite Jera in the calendar (Winter Solstice) and marks the beginning of the sun's seasonal demise.

With Othala in the position of second-to-last stave, preceding the time of Summer Solstice, there is an emphasis on closure and getting affairs in order. Dagaz is often attributed qualities of sunlight and clarity, given its associations with the balance of light and darkness. It's an eyes-open stave. Othala, however, is a time of eyes half-closed, a twilight of time and space in which we deal with our deceased kin.

Most often regarded as the stave used to call upon the Ancestors, it is indeed very useful for that purpose. Clan was the central focus of life in the Old Norse tradition. Everything that could affect the clan was deeply personal. The concept of being connected is at the fore. The way one behaved reflected on the entire clan, and this code was taken very seriously. Likewise precautions to protect the clan had very personal implications.

Othala's twilight quality brings up the concepts of innangard and utangard—the first being that which is known, the second being that which is beyond the boundary of what is known. Certainly clan was innangard, and wild territory beyond it was utangard. In the way that Mannaz challenged us to take a new idea into new territory, Othala demands that we understand personal twilight in all its depths. Where are we fed by our native surroundings, and where are we not? At what point is it worth leaving the innangard of the clan and venturing in to unknown utangard? Further, Othala emphasizes not just the legacy we are left but also what legacy we leave. Can we really know what legacy we leave without venturing into utangard? Aside from dealings with death and inheritance, ancestors and legacy, Othala brings a certain muted quality of somberness that, given our mastery of teachings of the runes leading up to this point, can lead to vivid insight into our life's meaning.

Another aspect of Othala is its connection to the three facets of Odin—warrior, shaman, wanderer. Having fought with himself and the world, then sacrificed himself to gain insight into örlög and wyrd, Odin realizes he is incapable of changing natural law and elects to remain as a guide for others so that they don't have to go through what he did. The aspect that Othala is associated with is the wanderer. Given that, in this season we consider what sacrifices were made for us to be where we are and what sacrifices we're willing to make for where we want to be. This of course means that we've decided that where we want to be is worth the sacrifice. Such is the level of responsibility of accounting with Othala.

Initiation is ultimately what Dagaz brings. At its heart is an opportunity to stand at the center of ourselves and All Things and draw down the Ancestors we've been working with, the wisdom of the work of this last of the sun's time, and mine from that wisdom what gives our lives meaning. Dagaz is heavy stuff, and in these two weeks it's framed in challenging company.

◆ DEVOTIONAL

Utangard and innangard describe the boundaries of the home space—what falls within it (*in*) and what falls without it (*út*). Just as the dwelling and the family's personal space fall within, so do certain favorable spirits—Land Elders, Nature Spirits (plants, trees, minerals, cardinal directions, consciousness of dwelling, Ancestors, and so forth). Likewise some spirits dwell without, such as other Nature Spirits, Land Elders, and anything we don't know.

The distinction of what is known versus unknown is more difficult for modern seekers than it was for our ancestors. Not having been raised in an animistic tradition, we don't have the benefit of elders who passed down this knowledge or the boundaries of in and out to us. We don't have stock definitions of beneficial spirits (clan totems or Ancestors) or beings that pose more challenge (such as collective Shadow or unquiet dead). We are left to explore that division with little (or no) time-tested wisdom as guidance. Yet we can't skip this component of Othala. It must be explored.

The organization of our home and our relationship to the Home Spirits determine how well we meet and deal with the diversity of the unknown. In this way Othala stresses the importance of having our home in order at deep levels. Part of the modern challenge of Othala is that we are less familiar with our known spiritual allies, which leaves us with less foundation to stand on as we explore parts unknown. The stronger our roots the more empowered we are when we venture into the wild.

In much the way you worked with Jera (Dream Team), Algiz (Home Spirits), and Ehwaz (Spirit Allies), now greet the Ancestors.

From a quiet space, indoors or out, call on All That You Are. Ask your Spirit Allies to remove any tension, thoughts, beliefs, or aspects that you no longer need to carry. Ask them to bring healing to specific areas, then to bring anything that you might need. After that, ask that they bring healing throughout you.

When you feel balanced in that exchange, ask that healing be directed from your spot in the present, through all lines of your ancestry, all the way back to the Source. Note any indications that specific family lines need attention. Observe where your understanding of "ancestry" may be challenged to include life-forms that aren't human, earthly, or comprehensible. Observe these, then set them aside for now.

If there are any particular personalities, features, or needs of your ancestral line, ask that your guides tend to them. Ask what ongoing tending needs to be done on your part, to take care of these specific needs, or to tend the line in general. Formulate a commitment to do what's asked of you. In this way you take deeper lessons into knowing, clearing, and weaving your wyrd.

Ask the Ancestors what they need from you.

Ask your Spirit Allies what they need from you.

As your work with Ancestors progresses during this half-month, realize that you are their future. Your present is the culmination of every choice made in your life. Such is the reality of Othala. This is All That You Are, fully present.

Othala Half-Month Affirmation

What came before,
What I do with now,
Is what I leave.

28
June 14–June 29
✦ Dagaz and Midsummer ✦
Befriending the Tension of Change

Summer Solstice occurs when the Earth is tilted most toward the sun. In the Northern Hemisphere this occurs between June 20 and 22. In the Southern Hemisphere it occurs between December 20 and 22. As a result of this tilt to the north, the sun's rays shine more directly over us, creating a longer days, hotter temperatures, and brighter spirits. This holy day marks the most dazzling display of solar power our life-giving star offers.

Going through our day-to-day lives we don't think much about the sun. We assume it will rise, we will plod through our schedule of events, only for the western horizon to tuck the sun back in at daylight's close. The sun is a key part of the scenery against which the action of our lives plays out.

In reality the sun is the most dramatic element in the story. Everything in our life revolves around it. Everything we have and hope to do is the result of the Earth's relationship with the sun. It's no surprise that for thousands of years Summer Solstice has marked a time of celebration, reminiscing, and rejoicing.

Because of the significance the sun plays in our lives, the solstice is a natural time to realize that we are part of the Earth-sun relationship, not just products of it. The challenge of paying that respect is that we only have one day in those blessed rays to do it. Luckily the days stretch longer this time of year, and we get the year's longest day to pay homage. It would seem there's plenty of time.

Our ability to celebrate what is light in our lives must also acknowledge that light isn't permanent. Seconds past the apex of Summer Solstice the sun's rays begin diminishing to winter. As soon as the sun is the brightest it can be, darkness begins creeping in. As soon as it reaches its highest angle, the sun's warmth cools. The days shorten, leaving us to sit with the truths that we can't conceive of brilliant light without also holding the shadows it casts. A day's sunlight won't last forever, and by default neither will we. It truly is our obligation to ourselves to make every day count.

Even though the sun continues to rise and set as the backdrop of our day, our experience of it shifts with the declining rays. Most of us don't need to panic the way that our ancestors did to make sure harvest is assured. Our psyches still experience that long-engrained need. Part of our task at Summer Solstice is to so vividly account for the blessings in our lives, such that our experience of accounting persists throughout the year.

Meaning "day," Dagaz is the stave of Summer Solstice. On the practical level, it's concerned with the micro harvest or accounting, making this rune wonderfully optimistic. Under all that brilliant sunlight it challenges us to honor what's good in our lives. I refer to Dagaz as the rune of hearth accounting, as it stands exactly opposite of Jera at midwinter, which emphasizes accounting for the year—a practice I call Hearth Accounting. The processes of these two staves are similar yet distinct.

Everything that one would normally employ to assess the success of a year Dagaz asks us to do in one day, each day, every day. Yet it isn't possible to hold all of that information at once. As a result we're forced to focus on only what matters most *each* day. It gives us the opportunity to realize what of each day had meaning, who we spent our time with, what was joyful, where we need more joy, how attitude affects all of the above. It asks us to impeccably determine what held meaning so that tomorrow can be created in support of more. Key with Dagaz is internal auditing, an intense inner exercise balanced by the solstice's guiding bright light.

That contrast sets up the spiritual framework of Dagaz and Summer Solstice. They open a sacred portal of initiation that can set the spiritual pace for the next year. Dagaz stands at precisely the midpoint between light and darkness, testing our comfort with betwixt space. It dredges up the tension of not being fully one thing or another. Few of us sit well with such uncertainty.

At the heart of any initiation is change. Every initiation reaches a point of crisis, by design. We tend to emphasize the light of Summer Solstice though the light is only defined by its shadow. Dagaz is light and darkness *that dwells in neither*. Its perfect poise doesn't last long, as we know that once its moment passes the days grow shorter. The moment passes, and we either complete the initiation or we don't.

The gift of Dagaz and Summer Solstice is the opportunity to stand in the center of ourselves and All Things, draw close our allies of the previous sun cycle, the wisdom of the work of the past year, and mine from them what gives our lives meaning.

Initiation left incomplete becomes post-traumatic stress. If working the Summer Solstice initiation at the time of its local alignment isn't possible, note the time that solstice occurs for your region and travel back to it through imagination to do this initiation.

◆ MIDSUMMER SABBAT INITIATION

About twenty minutes before the sun's rays are most direct for your location, begin this initiation. If necessary to shift into a more altered state, engage in fire breathing for a count of fifty. Breathing only through the mouth, close your eyes and inhale more deeply than usual, and exhale more deeply than usual, very quickly. Blow the breaths out forcefully, as if you are blowing them away from you. This style of breathing allows you to drop in to light trance quickly.

For this initiation find a quiet space that supports a quiet mind. If appropriate, gather fetishes and items of meaning and power to place about the space as you work. Turn off the phone, the television. If working outdoors, do so safely.

Imagine yourself in a pristine place in Nature, available only to you. Notice how it feels against your skin, what you hear, what aromas are carried on the breeze. As you take in the nuances of this space, ask your Spirit Allies to enter it with you. Feel the changes of the space as they enter; note the changes in your body and thoughts as they enter.

Call to the fore what within you needs to speak, and do so, aloud. It may be a supportive expression, it may be anger, joy, frustration, or a confluence of many feelings and states at once. Take this time, this moment betwixt, to honor all of self, no matter what comes. Suspend judgment or criticism of what comes, and just let it release. Give voice and compassion to all of you that must speak, particularly for the things you likely don't want to hear.

Speak until there is nothing left to say, then stand in the wisdom that you have heard yourself. You have honored the full presence of yourself.

As you speak pay attention from your crown to your throat, your chest to your belly button, your lower abdomen to the soles of your feet. Note the sensations, thoughts, memories, or beliefs that come up. This is how it feels to stand fully in yourself.

Bless the power. Bless the discomfort. Let both be.

Sing the galdr of Dagaz and note what feelings it stirs, what thoughts, emotions, and memories. Sense where the galdr rests in your body.

As you feel led in the stillness, bring your awareness back to your breathing. When you feel composed in your body, open your eyes.

This is how it feels to be fully present.

This is how it feels to welcome change without attempting to control it.

This is how it feels to have faith in yourself, in your natural process, and to be open to potential.

It's natural to feel rough edges after radical transformation. Allow them. Allow the myriad and possibly conflicting feelings to rise up and give them release the best way possible. Often it isn't the transformation that hammers us but the empty silence that follows. It's been a time of intense activity, within and without, so silence may seem a bit threatening.

Despite the harsh treatment, this isn't a time for creature comforts. As much as staying in bed for the rest of the week appeals, it will result in the loss of growth. Take walks in Nature. Talk when you can, and when you can't, breathe. Go out. Do. Be. Flex all the sore muscles carefully and with awareness of the new strength they bring.

Journal about your experience of Summer Solstice. Sit with how Dagaz presents in your life at this time, and record it. Keeping a journal of your initiations through the year serves not only as a chronicle of your experience but also becomes your personal lexicon of relating to the season and the staves.

As you write, consider the following:

Are you the same person at the dark of solstice as the one who rose at dawn? What has changed?

What makes one day unique from any other?

How do you celebrate repetition?

How do you honor diversity?

How can you carry the feelings of this solstice throughout the year?

> ### *Dagaz Half-Month Affirmation*
> Under the brightest light is truth,
> Shadowed only by my protection,
> Knowing my darkness is just as divine.

The candle flickers.

Rosemary burns.

On that faint light and smoke, the Ancestors come.

The mind quiets the heart, steps aside for the soul to rise.

Dagaz on this day, directly in line with the sun, begins all time, again. On this Summer Solstice, all twenty-four runes surround you in a perfect wheel. You are the directions, the spirits of space, and the intersection of time and timelessness. Through that joining, you find not meaning, purpose, above or below, in or out, but everything, All.

Yet you have not transcended yourself. You aren't on high with the holies, or without Shadow. You are ego-light and firmly grounded in your story, your flesh. In this center you stand, the axis to draw up wisdom and rain down actualization. Enlivened by the staves, you are the passionate youth and the wise elder around which wholeness spins, always.

29
Continuing the Cycle

I'm proud of you. It's not easy to follow through being led to initiation, let alone enduring and completing it. It's a scary process, because the need that leads us to it can't dictate where we will eventually go with it. That leap of faith is enormous, and I understand that by getting to this point in this journey, you're not the same person who first began reading this book.

Please take time to realize that for yourself.

Take time to sit with the changes that have come out of that process.

The truth of the cycle of initiations in this book is that they are the path to full personhood. They are what leads you from being the wounded child and the highly functioning adult to being a self-realized emotionally mature, inter-souled human capable of direct relationship with All Things to sustain self and show up for community.

The narrative of the seasonal runic initiations is they posit you in a new place, first ætt to the last, from which point you can no longer access the place where you began. Through the work done in daily devotionals and sabbat initiations, that place no longer exists to return to. Ultimately that release alone is why you stayed with them, it's the reason you completed them. Still, despite the desire, dedication, and success to become initiated, the result of it can feel raw and isolating.

Gather your resources and use them, on all levels. Do your personal casts. Spend time with Nature—not just in it but *with* it. Use the relationships the runes have opened to you. Go to your people, your witnesses, your teachers, your peers, your mentors. Sing to the spirits, and remember how each fits into your context through the runes. These are your allies. Continuing to work with your resources helps you sustain the teachings of your initiations and root their wisdom and teaching into All That You Are.

Don't forget—you can join the *Living the Runic Book of Days* Facebook community, where you can engage directly with me, share experiences, and continue living the calendar through the runes with others doing the same.

Most of all, the world needs people walking their walk, like you have through the study of this book. It needs people actively seeking direct relationship with the worlds in and about them so that the wyrd we work isn't just for our own benefit but that of all.

So thank you for walking this path of realized personhood, of direct revelation. Thank you for continuing your path of initiations, however they unfold, because we need you. The world needs you.

And of course, the nature of the runes through the seasons, as well as of humanity and life, is that we come to the end of one thing, only to be met by another. To that end, this cycle of initiations is designed so that you can repeat them annually, or even within some self-determined time frame. As you revisit the runic wheel you will be met with new challenges, new nuances of initiation, new aspects of self. However, because they are fixed on the wheel, you will also be greeted by the same allies, elements, and teachers as you meet new ones on every new journey.

This work is as big as it feels.

You did it.

You will continue doing it.

Thank you for that sacrifice.

Suggested Reading and Resources

Among my favorite rune resources are several wonderful books, websites, and personalities. Foremost among my favorites are Nigel Pennick's *Runic Astrology: Starcraft and Timekeeping in the Northern Tradition*, Freya Aswynn's *Northern Mysteries and Magick: Runes and Feminine Powers*, and Diana Paxson's *Taking Up the Runes: A Complete Guide to Using Runes in Spells, Rituals, Divination, and Magic*. You really can't go wrong with any books by these authors. Each offer a good base understanding of the runes with their personal twist, as well as innovations for how to work with the runes in a modern context.

Another favorite is Thomas Karlsson's *Uthark: Nightside of the Runes* (being rereleased in 2019 as *Nightside of the Runes: Uthark, Adulruna, and the Gothic Cabbla*). His is but one argument of an altered order for the Elder Futhark, albeit it is compelling enough that I agree.

Likewise every rune scholar needs to read the *Poetic Edda* and the *Prose Edda* by Snorri Sturluson. There are wonderful translations of these ancient texts, which are easily found online and in bookstores.

One of the most comprehensive websites on the runes is sunnyway .com/runes. This site covers the rich history, mythology, and cultural overtones of the Elder Futhark as well as shares insightful information on the Younger Futhark and the Anglo-Saxon Futhark.

The website norse-mythology.org, or Norse Mythology for Smart People, fills gaps in just about every aspect of Old Norse culture. This site offers thorough but approachable explanations of Old Norse terminology, key figures, and the general worldview of ancient Northern Europe.

There are also some great online video series, including the work of Maria Kvilhaug (theladyofthelabyrinth.com) and Sigha Manning. Search for both ladies on Youtube for primers on the runes, covering pronunciation, meaning, use, and history.

Finally I can't leave out the Youtube videos of Dr. Jackson Crawford. He is a professor of Old Norse studies who discusses every aspect of the Old Norse tradition and has a few focused videos on the Elder Futhark. His take is academic in a way that's refreshing amid the New Age romanticization of the runes.

Finally, you can find direct interaction with me and engagement with others learning about seasonal rune magick on the Facebook group for this book, Living the Runic Book of Days: www.facebook .com/groups/livingtherunicbookofdays. I also talk all things runes on my podcast, *What in the Wyrd,* and continue to publish *The Weekly Rune* at www.soulintentarts.com/runic.

Notes

INTRODUCTION

1. "Beowulf: An Anglo-Saxon Epic Poem," translated from the Heyne-Socin Text by John Lesslie Hall, Project Gutenberg eBook, www.gutenberg.org /files/16328/16328-h/16328-h.htm.

1. HISTORY AND ORIGIN OF THE RUNES

1. Patricia Terry, *Poems of the Elder Edda* (Philadelphia, Penn.: University of Pennsylvania Press, 1990), 31.
2. Edred Thorsson, *Futhark: A Handbook of Rune Magic* (Newburyport, Mass.; Weiser Books, 1984), 5.
3. Tineke Looijenga, *Texts and Contexts of the Oldest Runic Inscriptions* (Leiden and Boston: Brill, 2003), 9, 128.
4. Thorsson, *Futhark,* 1.
5. Raven Kaldera, *The Jotunbok: Working with the Giants of the Northern Tradition* (Hubbardston, Mass. Asphodel Press, 2006), 26.
6. Kaldera, *The Jotunbok,* 135.
7. Maria Kvilhaug, *The Seed of Yggdrasill: Deciphering the Hidden Messages in Old Norse Myths* (Denmark: Whyte Tracks, 2013), 4.
8. Varg Vikernes, *Germansk Mytologi Og Verdensanskuelse* (Sweden: Cymophane Publishing, 2000), 104.
9. Freya Aswynn, *Northern Mysteries and Magick: Runes and Feminine Powers* (Woodbury, Minn.: Llewellyn, 2002), 239.
10. Kaldera, *The Jotunbok,* 17.

2. THE RUNES

1. Paul Rhys Mountfort, *Nordic Runes: Understanding, Casting, and Interpreting the Ancient Viking Oracle* (Rochester, Vt.: Destiny Books, 2003), 12.

3. THE STAVES

1. Aswynn, *Northern Mysteries and Magick,* 54.
2. Thorsson, *Futhark,* 47.
3. Tacitus, *Germania*, chapter 2, https://facultystaff.richmond.edu/~wstevens /history331texts/barbarians.html.
4. Carl Sagan, *Cosmic Connection* (Cambridge, United Kingdom: Cambridge University Press), 22.

4. THE RUNIC CALENDAR

1. Aswynn, *Northern Mysteries and Magick,* 139.
2. Nigel Pennick, *Runic Astrology: Starcraft and Timekeeping in the Northern Tradition* (Northamptonshire, United Kingdom: The Aquarian Press, 1990), 158.
3. Pennick, *Runic Astrology,* 131.
4. Pennick, *Runic Astrology,* 131.
5. "Devotion," Online Etymology Dictionary, www.etymonline.com/index .php?term=devotion.
6. "Initiation," Dictionary.com, www.dictionary.com/browse/initiation?s=t.
7. Isaac Bonewits, "Varieties of Initiatory Experience," 1984 and 2005, www .neopagan.net/Initiation.html.

11. SEPTEMBER 28–OCTOBER 13
✦ GEBO ✦

1. *Hávamál: The Words of Odin the High One,* translated by Olive Bray, edited by D. L. Ashliman, verse 144, www.pitt.edu/~dash/havamal.html.

Glossary

Æsir: principle group of Old Norse gods and goddesses who reside in Asgard

ætt (pl. ættir): one of the three groups of eight runes in the Elder Futhark

Anglo-Saxon Futhark: a later runic group based on the Elder Futhark, also called the Anglo-Frisian Futhark

Asgard: the realm of the principle pantheon of Old Norse gods

Audhumla: feminine aspect of Nature in the form of a Giant aurochs, who fed the masculine aspect, giant Ymir, and sustained the original gods

Beltane: Celtic name for cross-quarter day between the Vernal Equinox and the Summer Solstice, celebrated around May 1; occurs when the sun reaches 15 degrees of Taurus; considered in many traditions to be the first day of summer

Bifröst: the Rainbow Bridge between the realms of Asgard and Midgard, guarded by Heimdallr

bind rune: a ligature of two or more runes

brightstave: an upright rune

Borr: Old Norse word for "son"; son of Buri and Bestla; father of Odin

Buri: also called Tyr or Tuisto, the first god in Old Norse mythology; the grandfather of Odin

cross-quarter days: the festivals of Lammas (August 1), Samhain (November 1), Imbolc (Febrary 1), and Beltane (May 1) all of which lie, more or less, at the midpoints between solstices and equinoxes

dísir: female ancestral spirits, honored at Yule

Disting: Norse name of the sabbat Imbolc (February 1)

Elder Futhark: the oldest form of the runic alphabet

Frey and Freya: Vanir twins taken as hostages of the Æsir; associated with the first ætt

futhark: a grouping of runes, so named from the first six characters of the Elder Futhark—f u th a r k

galdr: Old Norse for "spell" or "incantation; verbal or aural invocation of the runes

Ginnungagap: the void, from which All Things emerged

Gylfaginning: the first section of Snori Sturluson's *Prose Edda,* which recounts stories of the Norse gods

hamingja: spiritual aspect of oneself that oversees and affects personal luck

hamr: spiritual aspect of oneself that travels into astral planes to retrieve wisdom or healing

Hávamál: poem from the *Poetic Edda,* referencing Odin's wisdom, specifically how he retrieved the runes

Heimdallr: the guardian of the Rainbow Bridge

Huginn: one of Odin's ravens, meaning "thought"

Imbolc: the cross-quarter day between the Winter Solstice and the Vernal Equinox, celebrated February 1 or 2; occurs when the sun reaches 15 degrees of Aquarius; considered in many traditions to be the first day of spring

innangard: Norse term for "inside the gard," or what is known territory

Jötnar: plural of Jötun or the Old Norse race of giants; associated with the forces of Nature

Lammas: the cross-quarter day falling between the Summer Solstice and the Autumnal Equinox, celebrated on or about August 1; occurs when the sun reaches 15 degrees of Leo; also called Lughnasadh after the Celtic sun god Lugh; in the pagan wheel of the year Lammas is the first day of fall and the time of the first harvest, that of grains

Mabon: a Welsh word for the sabbat of the Autumnal Equinox and the days surrounding it; Mabon is the midpoint of autumn and the second harvest (fruits) of the fall season

magick: focused intent combined with action to change or create an outcome

merkstave: or "dark" stave; a reversed rune

Midgard: the human realm in Old Norse cosmology

Mjölnir: Thor's hammer

Multiverse: a reference to the nine worlds and the internal planes or states they evoke

Muninn: one of Odin's ravens, meaning "memory" or "desire"

Muspelheimr: the land of fire in the Old Norse creation myth

Niflheimr: the land of ice in the Old Norse creation myth

Nine Worlds: the nine realms that comprise the Old Norse cosmology— Asgard, Vanaheim, Midgard, Jotunheim, Alfheim, Svartalfheim, Niflheim, Muspelheim, and Hel

Nornir: or the Norns, the three sisters of wyrd in Norse mythology—Urd, Verdandi, and Skuld

Odin: primary god of the Old Norse pantheon; the Allfather and bearer of the runes to humanity

örlög: constraints and rules pertaining to our fate, including laws of Nature; aspects of fate that can't be changed

Ostara: named for a German goddess Eostre (whence Easter), Ostara is the sabbat of the Vernal Equinox, which is the midpoint of spring in the pagan calendar

Prose Edda: Old Norse literature written by Snorri Sturluson circa 1220 CE documenting Old Norse mythology

runecast: method of reading the runes in which they are tossed or cast onto a surface

runester: a modern-day proponent of the runes

sabbat: one of the eight holy days in the pagan calendar; the sabbats are the solstices, equinoxes, and the four cross-quarter days that lie at the midpoints between them

Samhain: the cross-quarter day between the Autumnal Equinox and the Winter Solstice, usually celebrated on November 1 or in the first week of November; occurs when the sun reaches 15 degrees of Scorpio;

Samhain is known as the third harvest (slaughter of animals) considered to be the first day of winter

seiðr: Old Norse shamanistic practice brought to the Æsir by Freya

Skáldskaparmál: the second part of Sturluson's *Prose Edda*

Sleipner: Odin's eight-legged horse, which carried him up Yggdrasil

Snorri Sturluson: author of the *Prose Edda*

stave: comes from the Icelandic Galdrastafir, which means magickal sticks; most often used when casting runes carved onto sticks rather than tiles, though in modern use is another name for a runic character

thurs: giant, jotun

Tyr: another name for the god Tuisto, or Buri

utangard: Norse term for "outside the gard," or what is unknown territory

Vanir: secondary group of Old Norse Nature gods and goddesses who reside in Vanaheim

Walpurgisnacht: in Germanic myth and folklore the culminating night of Walpurgis, the nine-night festival observation of Odin's ordeal on Yggdrasil; also known as Beltane

wyrd: from the Anglo-Saxon for "urd," tapestry of threads of personal and collective potentials, some of which we control and some we do not

wyrdweaving: intentional magickal shaping of one's personal wyrd, also of collective wyrd

Yggdrasil: the World Tree in Norse mythology; Odin hung from the tree for nine days and was given insight and the runes

Ymir: frost giant; masculine aspect of Nature, considered a creator of the original gods, with Audhumla

Index